This book is presented to

_____

It was given to you by

_____

Date

_____

My BIG Book of Bible
People, Places, and Things

Trust in the Lord
with all your heart

Almost everything in the Bible from A to Z

Phil A. Smouse

BARBOUR
PUBLISHING

For Sophie

With special thanks to Paul Muckley,
whose encouragement, support, and godly wisdom
made this book possible.

ISBN 978-1-60260-892-4

Published by Barbour Publishing, Inc., P.O. Box 719, Uhrichsville, Ohio 44683, www.barbourbooks.com

Our mission is to publish and distribute inspirational products offering exceptional value and biblical encouragement to the masses.

 Member of the
Evangelical Christian
Publishers Association

Printed in the United States of America.
RR Donnelley, Willard, OH 44890; March 2011; D10002693

A NOTE TO PARENTS

Do your kids have questions about the people, places, and things they read about in God's Word? This beautiful new reference book for children is packed with practical, fun, kid-friendly information on just about everything in the Bible.

With over 750 definitions, and nearly as many illustrations, *My Big Book of Bible People, Places, and Things* identifies the most important—and often most misunderstood—words, names, and phrases in scripture, then explains them in ways young readers can easily grasp.

Several key methods have been used to help children learn the meaning of each entry.

1. A simple explanation of the meaning of the word.
2. The use of the word in a sentence.
3. The use of the word and its synonym in two similar sentences.
4. The use of the word and its antonym.
5. A colorful picture illustrating the word or phrase.

Learning, understanding, and living God's Word is a journey that lasts a lifetime. Give your kids an important head-start with *My Big Book of Bible People, Places, and Things*. It's the fun way to understand God's Word!

AARON Aaron was **Moses' older brother**. Aaron helped Moses lead God's chosen people out of slavery and into the Promised Land.

Aaron **spoke the words** God gave to Moses. He told the king of Egypt to let God's people go!

Exodus 7–12

Aaron told Pharaoh to let God's people go!

ABBA Abba is a Bible word that means **"daddy."** God is our **heavenly Father**. We are His children. Because God loves us we can call Him daddy.

Romans 8:15

ABEDNEGO Shadrach, Meshach, and **Abednego** were **thrown into the fiery furnace** because they would not bow down and worship an idol. They would only worship God!

God protected the three friends. He kept them safe. They came out of the fire and did not get burned.

Daniel 3

ABEL   **Abel** was the second **son of Adam and Eve**. Abel loved God. But Abel's older brother, Cain, did not. Cain became jealous of Abel. He became so angry and bitter he killed his brother.

Genesis 4:1–15

ABIDE   Jesus said, "If you **abide** in Me, and My words **abide** in you, ask whatever you wish and it will be done for you." He said, "If you **live** in Me, and My words **live** in you, ask Me for anything, and I will do it."

John 15:7

ABRAHAM   **Abraham** was **God's friend.** He trusted God and did what God said even when it was very hard.

God asked Abraham to sacrifice his son, Isaac. Abraham did not want to sacrifice Isaac. But because Abraham trusted God, others learned to trust Him, too. Now God has more children than all the stars in the sky—and Abraham did not have to sacrifice His son!

Genesis 22:1–19

See also: Isaac, Sacrifice

ACACIA WOOD Acacia wood is the **sweet smelling, thorny wood** of the acacia tree.

The Ark that held God's Ten Commandments was a large box made of acacia wood.

Exodus 25:10

▲
Acacia tree

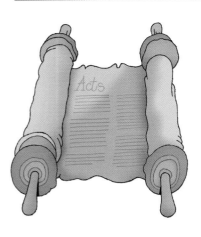

ACTS Acts is the name of a book in the New Testament. It is the name of a **book in the Bible**.

The book of Acts tells about the good things Jesus' friends and followers did and said. It tells how God's love grew and spread all over the world.

ADAM Adam was **the first man**.

God made Adam. He formed Adam's body from the dust of the earth. God breathed life into Adam's body and Adam became alive!

Genesis 2:7

Adder – Agape

ADDER   An **adder** is a biting **snake** whose sharp teeth are filled with poison. It is a **long, thin animal** with no legs that crawls along the ground.

Isaiah 59:5

ADONAI   **Adonai** is a Bible word that means **Lord and master**. Jesus is our Adonai. We belong to Him.

Isaiah 61:1

ADOPTED   We have been **adopted** by Jesus. Jesus **took us into His family** and made us His own.

Galatians 3:26; Ephesians 1:5

AGAPE   **Agape** is a Bible word that means **love**.

God is **agape**. God is **love**. God loves us so much He gave His only Son to take our sins away.

John 3:16; 1 John 4:8

AIJALON   Joshua fought a **great battle** in the **Valley of Aijalon**. When he prayed, God made the sun and the moon stand still in the sky until the battle was over and God's children had won.

Joshua 10:12–13

The sun stands still over Aijalon ➤

ALABASTER   The woman has an **alabaster** jar filled with perfume. She has a jar made of **beautiful smooth, white stone**.

Luke 7:37–38

ALLELUIA   The people shouted, **"Alleluia!"** The people shouted, **"Praise the Lord!"**

Revelation 19:6

ALMIGHTY   God is **Almighty**. He is **more powerful than anything or anyone**.

Psalm 24

10

ALPHA AND OMEGA

Alpha is a Bible word that means **first or beginning**.
Omega is a Bible word that means **last or ending**.

Jesus said, "I am the **Alpha and the Omega**."

He said, "I am the first and the last, the **beginning**
and the **ending**. I was alive before the world began.
And I will be alive even when it comes to an end!"

Revelation 1:8

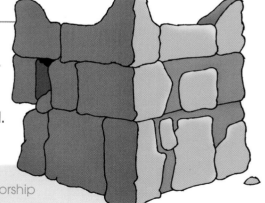

ALTAR Abraham built an **altar**
out of stones. He piled up stones
to make a **place to worship God**.

Genesis 22:9

See also: Horns of the Altar, Sacrifice, Worship

AMEN After she prayed we all said, **"Amen!"** When she
was finished praying we all said, **"Yes, Lord Jesus! Let it be!"**

Jude 25

ANAKITE The **Anakite** people were **giants**. They were tall, strong, and very mean to the Children of Israel.

Numbers 13:33; Deuteronomy 9:2–3

See also: Twelve Spies

An Anakite giant! ➤

ANANIAS AND SAPPHIRA Ananias and Sapphira were believers who **lied to God** and **lied to their friends**. They did not tell the truth. God was very angry at Ananias and Sapphira for not telling the truth.

Acts 5:1–10

ANCIENT OF DAYS Daniel had a special name for God. He called God the **Ancient of Days**.

Daniel knew God has always been—and will always be— **alive forever and ever!**

Daniel 7:9

Daniel knew God was amazing! ➤

Andrew – Anoint

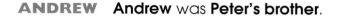

ANDREW **Andrew** was **Peter's brother.**

He and Peter were fishermen. They were also Jesus' disciples. Andrew and Peter helped spread the good news about Jesus all over the world!

Matthew 4:18–20

See also: Disciple, Peter

ANGEL **Angels** are **God's messengers.** God sends His angels from heaven to help us and to tell us what to do.

Genesis 22:11–12; Luke 2:9–14

ANOINT Moses will **anoint** Aaron with oil. He will **pour oil** on Aaron's head.

Moses will dedicate Aaron's life to God. He will show everyone Aaron loves God and wants God to use him to help others.

Exodus 29:7

ANOINTING OIL Anointing oil is a **sweet-smelling perfume or lotion**.

It is made from cinnamon, myrrh, olive oil, and other spices.

Exodus 30:22–25

ANTICHRIST A man who will come and **pretend to be God** is called the **Antichrist**.

The Antichrist will say Jesus is not God's son. He will try to sit on God's throne. The Antichrist will try to get rid of God once and for all. But God will get rid of him!

2 Thessalonians 2:3–4, 8; 1 John 2:22

ANTIOCH Barnabas and Saul traveled to **Antioch** to tell the people about Jesus.

They went to a large **town north of Jerusalem** where the people who followed Jesus were first called Christians.

Acts 11:25–26

APOSTLE   A person Jesus chose to **tell people about God's love** was called an **apostle**. The apostles shared all the amazing things Jesus said and did with everyone they met.

Matthew 10:2–4; Mark 3:14

ARK OF THE COVENANT   The **Ark of the Covenant** is a **large box made of acacia wood**. The Ark had two angels carved on its top. It was **covered with gold**.

The Ark was made by God's children **to hold the Ten Commandments**. It also held Aaron's staff and a jar of manna.

Exodus 25:10–22; Hebrews 9:4

ARMAGEDDON   The **last battle between good and evil** will be fought the Valley of **Armageddon**. The Valley of Armageddon is in the land of Israel near Jesus' boyhood home of Nazareth.

Revelation 16:16

ASHERAH POLE   Gideon cut down the **Asherah pole**. He cut down the **wooden statue of a false god** and burned it in a fire.

Judges 6:25–26

ASHES   Job sat down on the ground and covered himself with **ashes**. He covered himself with the **gray powder left behind when something burns**. Job put ashes on his head to show God he was sorry for the bad things he did and he wanted to change.

Job 2:7–9

ASP   The **asp** hid near the river among the lotus blossoms and reeds. The **small, poisonous snake** hid among the flowers and reeds.

Isaiah 11:8

ASSURANCE   Because we trust in Jesus, we have the **assurance** we are saved. We **know without a doubt** everyone who calls on the name of the Lord will be saved.

Romans 10:9–10

Baal – Babylon

BAAL   **Baal** was a **false god**. Baal was a make-believe god people worshipped instead of the One True God.

Judges 2:13

BABEL, TOWER OF   The people of Babylonia tried to build the **Tower of Babel**. They tried to make a tall **building that reached all the way to heaven.**

But the people of Babylon did not love or worship the One True God. So God made them all speak in different languages.

No one could understand what anyone was saying, so they could not finish the Tower of Babel.

Genesis 11:1–9

BABYLON   **Babylon** was a **large, beautiful city** between two rivers. It was the capital of Babylonia. Daniel was thrown into the lion's den by the king of **Babylon**.

Jeremiah 50; Daniel 6

A
B
C
D
E
F
G
H
I
J
K
L
M
N
O
P
Q
R
S
T
U
V
W
X
Y
Z

Bb

BALAAM   **Balaam** was a **prophet with a talking donkey**.

The king of Moab wanted Balaam to curse God's people. He wanted Balaam to ask a false god to make God's people suffer.

But God made Balaam's donkey speak. So Balaam blessed God's people instead!

Numbers 22–24

BALM   The doctor put **balm** on a patient. The doctor put a **good-smelling cream** on a patient to make him feel better.

Jeremiah 8:22

BAPTIZED   The disciples **baptized** many people. They **dipped them in the water** to show everyone Jesus washed their sins away.

Matthew 3

Barabbas – Barnabas

BARABBAS **Barabbas** was a **criminal**. He did many bad things. Barabbas was in prison when Jesus was arrested.

Pilate wanted to set Jesus free. But the religious leaders wanted Jesus to die. "Give us Barabbas!" they shouted. So Pilate listened to the people. He set Barabbas free and punished Jesus instead!

Mark 15:1–15

See also: Jesus, Pilate

BARLEY **Barley** is a **cereal** like wheat, oats, or rye. A farmer grows barley to feed his farm animals. Some people who were very poor used barley to make bread.

Ruth 1:22; 1 Kings 4:28; John 6:9

Barley ➤

BARNABAS **Barnabas** was a **missionary**. Barnabas helped his friend Paul tell people about Jesus.

Acts 11:22–26

BARTIMAEUS, BLIND   **Bartimaeus** was a **blind beggar**. He had no food or money and could not see.

"What do you want?" Jesus asked. "I want to see," Bartimaeus replied. So Jesus touched his eyes and Bartimaeus could see!

Mark 10:46–52

BASIN   Jesus picked up a **basin** and began to wash Peter's feet. He picked up a **wide, shallow bowl** filled with water and began to wash Peter's feet.

John 13:2–5

BATHSHEBA   **Bathsheba** was **king Solomon's mother**. She was a very beautiful woman. King David wanted Bathsheba to be his wife. But Bathsheba was already married. So David did a terrible thing!

He made sure Bathsheba's husband died in battle then married her himself. But God saw what David did. He was very angry and punished David for it.

2 Samuel 11–12

BEARD   Barzillai has a big, fuzzy **beard**.

He has **hair growing on his cheeks and underneath his chin**.

Psalm 133:1–3

BEATITUDES   The **Beatitudes** are part of a **sermon Jesus preached**. The Beatitudes teach us how to be happy. People are happy when they live the way God wants them to live.

Matthew 5:1–12

BEGGAR   Peter healed the **beggar** who sat at the city gate. He healed the **man who asked people to give him money or food**.

Acts 3

BEHEMOTH   The **behemoth** was a **large plant-eating animal**. It had strong legs, a powerful body, and a long, thick tail.

The behemoth lived near the water. It liked to hide among the trees and reeds.

Job 40:15–24

BELIEVER   Ruthie is a **believer**. She believes **Jesus is the living Son of the One True God**. She trusts Jesus with all her heart and knows every word God says is true.

Acts 2:42–47

BELSHAZZAR   **Belshazzar** was a **king in Babylon**. Belshazzar saw God's hand write on a wall.

Daniel told Belshazzar what the writing meant. Belshazzar would lose his kingdom that night.

Daniel 5

BENJAMIN **Benjamin** was **Joseph's baby brother**. He was the son of Jacob and Rachel. Benjamin's older brothers were jealous of Joseph's coat of many colors. They were very angry because Joseph had a beautiful coat and they did not.

Genesis 35:16–18, 43:29

See also: Coat of Many Colors, Joseph

BETHANY **Bethany** is a **village on the Mount of Olives** near Jerusalem. Jesus raised Lazarus from the dead in the village of Bethany.

John 11:1–44

See also: Jerusalem, Lazarus, Mount of Olives

BETHEL **Bethel** is a **very old town** in the land of Judea. The name *Bethel* means "house of God."

Jacob had a dream in Bethel. Jacob saw angels on stairs that went up to heaven.

Genesis 28:10–19

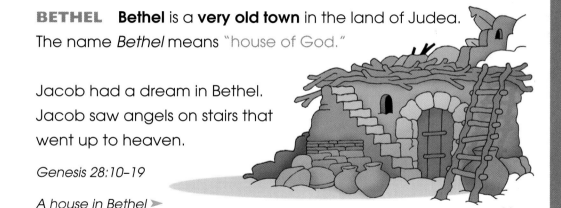

A house in Bethel ➤

BETHLEHEM   Jesus was born in **Bethlehem**. He was born in a **little town just south of Jerusalem** in the land of Israel. Mary and Joseph walked almost one hundred miles from Nazareth to Bethlehem.

Luke 2:1–4

BETRAY   One of the twelve disciples will **betray** Jesus. One of the twelve will **pretend to be a friend then help Jesus' enemies**. Because He was betrayed, Jesus will be captured and nailed to the cross.

Mark 14:18

BIBLE   The **Bible** is **God's Word**.

God helped people write His words into books. Sixty-six books make up the Bible. The Bible is sometimes called scripture.

2 Timothy 3:16

See also: Scripture

Bildad – Bitumen

BILDAD   **Bildad** was **one of Job's friends**. Bildad's friend Job was very sad. Many bad things happed to Job. Bildad tried to make Job feel better by saying things that sounded helpful and smart.

But Bildad's words were not God's words. So the things Bildad said only made Job feel worse!

Job 2:11, 8:1–22

BIRTHRIGHT   Esau sold his **birthright** for a bowl of stew. He gave away the **good things that belonged to him because he was his father's firstborn son**.

Genesis 25:33

BITUMEN   Moses' mother covered the little basket with **bitumen** and pitch. She covered the basket with **sticky, black tar** so it would not leak.

Exodus 2:3

A basket covered with bitumen ➤

BLASPHEME We should never **blaspheme** God. We should never **say bad things** about God.

Leviticus 24:15–16

BLESS Jesus loves to **bless** His children. He loves to **give us every good thing** when we love and trust Him with all our heart.

Proverbs 10:6, 22; Romans 4:8, 10:12

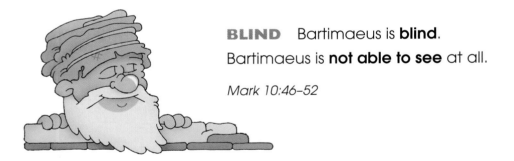

BLIND Bartimaeus is **blind**. Bartimaeus is **not able to see** at all.

Mark 10:46–52

BLOOD OF JESUS The **blood of Jesus** washes away all our sins. **Because Jesus died** on the cross, **we are forgiven** forever!

1 John 1:7

Boaz – Bold

BOAZ **Boaz** was **Ruth's husband**. He was her kinsman-redeemer.

Boaz took care of Ruth and her mother-in-law, Naomi, when they had nowhere else to turn.

Ruth and Boaz were the great-grandparents of King David. King David was the ancestor of *King Jesus!*

Ruth 4:13–17

See also: Kinsman-Redeemer, Naomi, Ruth

BODY OF CHRIST We are the **Body of Christ**. We are the **people who love Jesus** and have been **born again**.

1 Corinthians 12:27

See also: Born Again, Church

BOLD Joshua was **bold** and strong. He was **brave, fearless, and trusted God** at all times.

Joshua 1:6–9

A
B
C
D
E
F
G
H
I
J
K
L
M
N
O
P
Q
R
S
T
U
V
W
X
Y
Z

BONDAGE   The Children of Israel were in **bondage** to Pharaoh. He would not let God's people go. The king of Egypt **held them against their will** and **forced them to be slaves**.

Exodus 1:8–14

BOOK OF LIFE   The names of God's children are kept in the **Book of Life**. The Book of Life is a **list of names** of people who are saved.

Revelation 21:27

BORN AGAIN   Jesus said, "You must be **born again**." He said you must **let Me come and live** deep down **in your heart**.

John 3:7, 16–17

HOW MUCH?

God loved the world so much He gave His only Son so whoever believes in Him will never die, but will live with God in heaven *forever*.

Bowstring – Breastplate

BOWSTRING   A **bowstring** is the strong, flexible **string on an archer's bow**. The archer puts an arrow against the string, pulls back, and lets his arrow fly.

Psalm 21:12

BREAD OF LIFE   Do you have a hungry heart? Jesus said, "I am the **Bread of Life**." When you come to **Jesus** and give your heart to Him, it will never, ever be hungry again.

John 6:30–35

BREASTPLATE   The high priest wore a **breastplate**.

He wore a **special piece of clothing** over his heart.

The breastplate was made with gold and twelve different jewels.

Exodus 28:15–30

BRIDE   Ruth and Boaz are getting married today. Ruth is the **bride**. She is a **woman on her wedding day**.

Isaiah 62:5

BRIDE OF CHRIST   We are **God's children**. God's children are the church. The church is the **Bride of Christ**.

Ephesians 5:25–32; Revelation 19:7

BRIDEGROOM   Boaz and Ruth are getting married today. Boaz is the **bridegroom**. He is a **man on his wedding day**.

Isaiah 61:10

BRIDLE   The children helped the farmer put on the horse's **bridle**. They helped him put on the **straps and buckles** that go over the horse's head, neck, and ears.

Psalm 32:9

A horse wearing a bridle ➤

BRONZE Bronze is a **yellow-brown metal**. Bible people made tools and weapons from bronze. They also used bronze to make beautiful decorations.

Genesis 4:22

BROOD The bunny hid her **brood** in a hole underneath the broom tree. She hid her **family of young animals** in a hole underneath the tree.

Matthew 12:34

BROOM TREE Elijah sat under the **broom tree**. He sat under a **prickly little tree with bright yellow flowers**.

1 Kings 19:4

◄ *Elijah under the broom tree*

31

Bb

BULLOCK The farmer took a **bullock** to the temple for the offering. He took a **young male cow** for the offering.

Exodus 29:36

See also: Burnt Offering, Offering

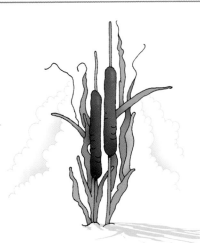

BULRUSHES Moses' mother made a basket from **bulrushes**.

She made a basket from **tall plants,** like cattails, **that grow near the water**.

Exodus 2:1–3

BURNING BUSH Moses heard God's voice speaking to him from inside the **Burning Bush**.

The Lord appeared to Moses in the flames of a **bush that was on fire but did not burn up**. God told Moses to go to Egypt and tell Pharaoh to let His people go!

Exodus 3

Burnish – Burnt Offering

BURNISH   The artist **burnished** the cups and bowls for the temple. He **made the surface smooth and shiny** by rubbing it with a special tool.

1 Kings 7:45

◄ *A burnishing tool*

BURNT OFFERING   The priest prepared a **burnt offering** as a gift to God to cover the sins of the people.

He took the **fat, inner parts, head, and legs of a healthy male animal** and burned them in a smoky fire.

Leviticus 1:7–9

A priest placing a burnt offering upon the altar ▲

CAESAR Caesar is a title for the **ruler of the Roman Empire**. It is a special name for the leader of the Roman Empire.

Luke 2:1

CAIAPHAS Caiaphas was the **High Priest of Israel**. He was the religious leader of God's people.

Because Jesus said He was God's son, Caiaphas said Jesus should die.

Matthew 26:3–5, 62–66

See also: High Priest

CAIN Cain was the first **son of Adam and Eve**. Cain became jealous of his younger brother Abel. He became angry and bitter because Abel loved God and he did not.

Cain became so angry he **killed his brother Abel**.

Genesis 4:1–15

See also: Abel, Adam, Eve

Caleb – Calling

CALEB **Caleb** was **one of the twelve spies** Moses sent to take the Promised Land. Ten spies were afraid to try. The land was filled with giants!

But Caleb was not afraid. He said, "We should go up and take the land." "We can surely do it."

Numbers 13–14; Joshua 14:6–12

See also: Joshua, Moses, Promised Land

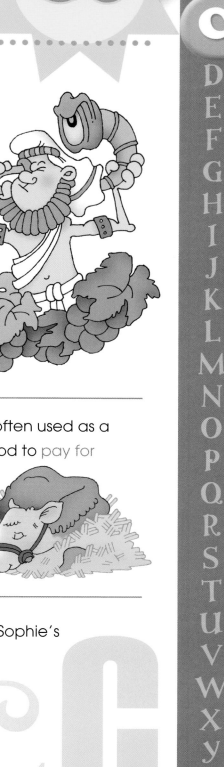

CALF A **calf** is a **young cow**. Calves were often used as a sacrifice to God. A calf would be given to God to pay for people's sins.

Leviticus 9:8

See also: Sacrifice

CALLING Teaching people about Jesus is Sophie's **calling**. It is **the thing God created her to do**.

2 Thessalonians 1:11

CALVARY   Jesus died on the cross at **Calvary**.
He died on a **hill just outside the city of Jerusalem**.

Luke 23:33

See also: Crucify, Golgotha, Resurrection

CAMEL   Abram rode a **camel** through the desert.

He rode a large, long necked **animal** with humps on its back.

Camels can live a long time without food or water.

Genesis 24:11

CAMP   God's people set up **camp** when they traveled.
They picked a **place to put up their tents**.

Exodus 14:19–20

A camp in the desert ➤

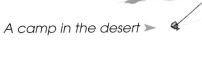

CANA   Jesus did his first miracle at **Cana**. Jesus turned water into wine in a **small town in Galilee**.

John 2:1–11

CANAAN   God told Abram to leave his home and go to the land of **Canaan**.

He told Abram to go to the **Promised Land**.

Genesis 15:18

See also: Promised Land

Abram on his way to Canaan ▲

CAPERNAUM   Jesus lived in **Capernaum**. He lived in a **village on the shore of the Sea of Galilee**. Andrew, Peter, Matthew, James, and John also lived in Capernaum.

Matthew 4:13

See also: Galilee

CAPTIVITY God's people were taken into **captivity**. God's people were made **prisoners in another country**.

2 Kings 24:15

CEDARS OF LEBANON Solomon built God's temple with the **cedars of Lebanon**.

He built it with **strong, tall pine trees** that grew in beautiful green forests on the mountains and hills of Lebanon.

1 Kings 5:6

See also: Temple

CENSER Eleazar burned incense in a bronze **censer**.

Eleazar used a **little metal jar** to burn fine powder that makes sweet-smelling smoke.

Leviticus 16:12; Numbers 4:16

CENSUS Moses took a **census** of all the people. He **counted all the people** to see how many there were.

Numbers 1:2

CENTURION A **centurion** was a **soldier from the Roman Empire**.

Centurions were leaders of one hundred other soldiers.

Matthew 8:5–9

A Roman centurion ➤

CHAFF God's enemies are like **chaff** blown away by the wind. His enemies are blown away like the worthless **dust of chopped grain, hay, or straw.**

Psalm 1:4

CHARIOT The Pharaoh of Egypt rode in a **chariot**.

He rode in a **cart with two wheels pulled by a horse**.

Exodus 14:6

CHARIOT OF FIRE Elijah went to heaven in a **chariot of fire**.

He went in a **cart pulled by fiery horses** that blazed like the sun but did not burn up.

2 Kings 2:11

CHERUBIM **Cherubim** are **angels with wings**. Cherubim kept Adam and Eve away from the Garden of Eden after they sinned.

Genesis 3:24

Chief Priests – Chosen People

CHIEF PRIESTS The **chief priests** wanted to find a way to kill Jesus.

The **religious leaders** of the children of Israel wanted Jesus to die.

Matthew 26:59

CHILDREN OF ISRAEL The **Hebrew people** are sometimes called the **Children of Israel**. The children of Israel are Jacob's sons whose families became the twelve tribes of Israel.

Exodus 1:7

CHOSEN PEOPLE We are God's **chosen people**. We are the **people who belong to Jesus**.

Jesus took us out of the darkness of our sin. He brought us into the wonderful light of His love.

Colossians 3:11–12; 1 Peter 2:9

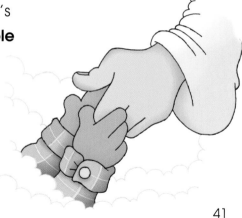

CHRIST   **Christ** is a title for **Jesus**. It is a special name for God's Son. *Christ* means "the anointed one." Jesus was chosen by God to save people from sin.

Matthew 1:16

CHRISTIAN   Sophie is a **Christian**. She **loves Jesus with all her heart**.

She believes what Jesus says and wants to follow Him wherever He goes.

2 Corinthians 5:17; 1 Peter 4:16

CHURCH   We are the **Church**. We are **God's children**.

Jesus is alive in our hearts. We have been born again.

Matthew 16:18

CISTERN   Reuben stores water in a **cistern**. He stores water in a deep **hole in the ground**.

Proverbs 5:15

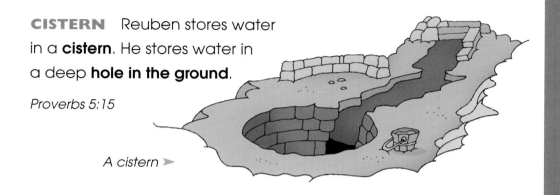

A cistern ➤

CITY GATE   When the sun goes down it will be time to close the **city gate**.

It will be time to close the **large door built into the wall** that goes all the way around the city.

Joshua 2:5

CITY OF DAVID   Jesus was born in **Bethlehem**. He was born in the **City of David**.

Luke 2:4

COAT OF MANY COLORS Jacob made his son Joseph a **coat of many colors**. He made Joseph the **most beautiful coat** he or his brothers had ever seen.

Joseph's brothers were very jealous of Joseph's beautiful coat.

Genesis 37:3

See also: Israel, Jacob, Joseph

COCK A **cock** is a **rooster**. A rooster likes to crow early in the morning. Jesus told Peter, "Before the cock crows you will deny Me three times."

Matthew 26:34

COLT A **colt** is a **young male horse or donkey**. Jesus rode a colt into Jerusalem.

Matthew 21:2

Comforter – Compassion

COMFORTER   Jesus said He would send the **Comforter**. He would send God's **Holy Spirit** to help us, teach us, and show us the truth.

John 14:16

See also: Holy Spirit

COMMANDMENTS God gave His people many **commandments**.

He gave His people **rules to follow and obey**.

Exodus 20:1–17

See also: Ten Commandments

Moses with God's Ten Commandments ➤

COMPASSION   Jesus showed **compassion** to the people around Him. Jesus was **kind and helpful to people in need**.

Matthew 9:36

CORBAN   The Pharisee's mother and father were poor and needed money. But the Pharisee did not want to give money to his mother and father.

"I can not give you this money," the religious man said. "This money is **Corban**. It is a **gift for God alone**."

Mark 7:9–13

See also: Pharisee

CORINTH   The apostle Paul lived and taught in **Corinth**. He lived and taught God's Word in a **large Greek city beside the sea**.

Acts 18:1

CORNERSTONE   Jesus is our **cornerstone**. He is the first and **most important piece of our lives**.

Every good thing we have is built on, supported, and held together by Jesus' love.

Ephesians 2:19–22

Courage – Covenant

COURAGE Joshua was a man of **courage**.
He was **brave and fearless** in dangerous times.

Joshua 1:9

COURTYARD
Peter sat in the **courtyard** and warmed himself by the fire.

He sat in the **outside area of a large building surrounded by walls and open to the sky**.

Mark 14:66

COVENANT God said, "I will make a **covenant** with you. I will make a **promise that can never be broken**."

Exodus 34:10; Matthew 26:28

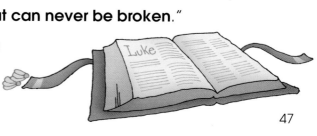

COVET God says not to **covet** the things your friends have. He says do not **wish you had those things** so much that you would sin to get them.

Deuteronomy 5:21

CREATED In the beginning God **created** the heavens and the earth. God **made something real where there was nothing before**.

Genesis 1:1

God created the heavens and the earth!

CREATION "Go into all the world and preach the good news to all **creation**." Go and tell **everyone and everything God has ever made** about Jesus.

Mark 16:15

A B C D E F G H I J K L M N O P Q R S T U V W X Y Z

Creator – Crown

CREATOR God is the **creator** of all things. God is **the one who made our world and everything in it**.

Genesis 14:19; Isaiah 40:28

CROSS Jesus was nailed to a **cross** to take away our sins. His hands and feet were nailed to a **rough wooden post shaped like a *T***.

Matthew 27:11–56

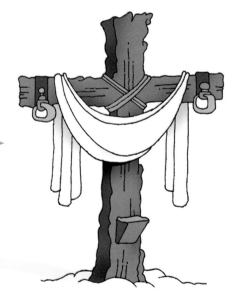

Jesus died on the cross at Calvary ➤

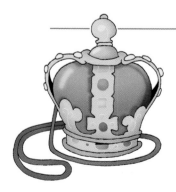

CROWN A **crown** is a special **head covering worn by kings and queens**. Crowns are often made of gold and jewels.

Esther 2:17

CROWN OF THORNS The soldiers placed a **crown of thorns** on Jesus' head.

They twisted **small branches with many stiff, sharp points** into a circle and pressed it down hard on Jesus' head.

Matthew 27:29

CRUCIFY The people all shouted, "**Crucify** him. Crucify him!" They shouted, "**Nail Him to a cross and leave Him to die!**"

Luke 23:21

CUBIT A **cubit** is a **measure of length** like an inch, a foot, a yard, or a mile. One cubit is about the size of a grown man's arm from the end of his elbow to the tip of his fingers.

Genesis 6:15

CUPBEARER Nehemiah was a **cupbearer** for the king. He **tasted the king's drinks to make sure they were safe**.

Nehemiah 1:11

Dd

A B C **D** E F G H I J K L M N O P Q R S T U V W X Y Z

DAILY BREAD Jesus will give us our **daily bread**.

He will give us **everything we need to live** each and every day.

Matthew 6:11

Food is one kind of daily bread ➤

DAMASCUS ROAD Saul became a Christian on the **Damascus Road**. He became a believer when he heard Jesus' voice on the **road between Damascus and Jerusalem**.

Acts 9:1–31

DANIEL

Daniel was a **prophet**. Daniel **told people about God**. He told them what God wanted them to do.

Daniel was very wise. God showed him what would happen to His people in the future. Daniel could even tell people the meaning of their dreams.

Daniel 1–12

A B C D E F G H I J K L M N O P Q R S T U V W X Y Z

Dd

DARIUS   **Darius** was a **title** given to certain kings in the Bible. It was a special name given to those kings.

Darius the Mede threw Daniel into the lion's den.

Daniel 6:1–23

DARKNESS   Without the sun we would be in **darkness**.

Without the sun we would have **no light at all**.

Exodus 10:21–23

OUT OF THE DARKNESS

A heart without God's love is like a man who is lost in the darkness.

He can't tell where he is. He doesn't know where he is going. And without the light of God's Word, he won't ever find the way out.

God's Word is the light that will chase darkness away. Let Jesus lead you out of the darkness and into God's wonderful light. *(1 Peter 2:9)*

DAVID **David** grew up to become the **king of Israel**. He was the ruler of God's people.

David was born in Bethlehem. He used a slingshot and a stone to kill the giant Goliath. He was a shepherd, a musician, and a man after God's own heart.

1 Samuel 17:20–58

DAY STAR The **day star** is a bright, early **morning star**. You can see it just before the sun begins to shine.

Revelation 22:16

DEAD SEA The **Dead Sea** is a very **salty lake in Israel**. Water flows in, but it does not flow out. The Dead Sea has too much salt for plants or animals to live and grow.

Ezekiel 47:6–12

DEAF My friend Charles is **deaf**. My friend Charles **cannot hear**.

Matthew 11:5

DEATH   Even when I walk through the valley of the shadow of **death** God will be with me. God will always be with us, even at **the end of our lives**.

John 5:24

DEBTOR   The servant asked to speak with his master's **debtors**. He asked to speak with people who **borrowed his master's money and had not yet paid it back**.

Matthew 6:12; Luke 16:5; Romans 13:8

THUS
SAYS
THE
LORD

DECREE   A **decree** is a **king's command**.

Mary and Joseph went to Bethlehem because of a king's decree. God is the most important king. He makes decrees, too.

Luke 2:1–5

DEEDS   I will tell everyone about God's love and good **deeds**. I will tell everyone about God's love and the good **things He says and does**.

Psalm 107:8

Delilah – Deliverer

DELILAH   Samson was a mighty man of God. His long hair gave him power and strength.

Samson fell in love with **Delilah**. But Delilah did not love Samson. She tricked him!

She set a trap and **cut off Samson's hair**. Then his power and strength were gone. Samson's enemies captured him and took him away.

Judges 16

See also: Samson

DELIVERER   Jesus is our **deliverer**. Jesus is the one who **sets us free from** the chains of **sin**.

Romans 11:26

DEMON   A **demon** is a **helper of the devil**. Demons cause trouble for people. They try to keep people from God.

Romans 8:37–39

DENARIUS   The vineyard owner gave each worker a **denarius**.

He gave each worker one **small silver coin** worth about a day's pay.

Matthew 20:2

See also: Vineyard

DESERT   Moses led the people through the **desert**. He led them through a **dry, empty land covered with sand**.

Exodus 15:22

Devil – Diadem

DEVIL   Another name for **Satan** is the **devil**.

The devil wants to hurt God's children. He wants to make them do bad things.

Worst of all, the devil wants everyone to think God's Word is not true. But Jesus said the devil is a liar. He said the devil is the father of lies. He said there is no truth in him.

John 8:44; Revelation 12:9

DEW   Dew is **water in the nighttime air**. At night, dew makes things wet. God used the dew to answer questions from a soldier named Gideon.

Judges 6:36–40

DIADEM   Aaron was a priest. He wore special robes and a turban with a **diadem**.

A diadem ➤

He wore a **headband** around his turban covered with pure gold.

Exodus 29:5–7, 39:30

Dd

DISCIPLES   Peter, Andrew, James, and John were **disciples** of Jesus. They were people who **loved Jesus and followed Him wherever He would go**.

The disciples spread the good news about Jesus all over the world.

Matthew 10:2–4

THE TWELVE DISCIPLES

Peter
Andrew (Peter's brother)
James and John
(the sons of Zebedee)
Philip
Bartholomew
Thomas
Matthew the tax collector
James, son of Alphaeus
Thaddaeus
Simon the Zealot
Judas Iscariot, who betrayed Jesus

Donkey – Dream

DONKEY   When Balaam's **donkey** saw an angel, she ran off the road and into a field.

A donkey is a **gray animal that looks like a small horse**. Donkeys have long ears and like to say, "hee-haw!"

Numbers 22:23

DOVE   A **dove** is a **gentle bird**. The Bible says God's Spirit is like a dove. People saw the Spirit come down on Jesus after He was baptized.

Matthew 3:16

DREAM   God spoke to Jacob in a **dream**.

He gave Jacob a special message, like a movie, with **thoughts and pictures that passed through his mind while he slept**.

Jacob dreamed about angels and a stairway that went all the way to heaven.

Genesis 28:10–16

A B C D E F G H I J K L M N O P Q R S T U V W X Y Z

DROUGHT   A **drought** is a very **long time with no rain at all**.

Jeremiah 17:8

DUMB   Jesus healed the man who was **dumb**. He healed the man who was **not able to speak**.

Mark 7:37

DUSK   **Dusk** is a **time of night**.

Dusk is the time just before the night is at its darkest.

1 Samuel 30:17

Demetrius taking a walk at dusk ➤

DUST   God made Adam from the **dust** of the earth. God took a handful of **soft, dry, powdery dirt** and breathed life into it. Adam came alive!

Genesis 2:7

Eden – Egypt

EDEN **Eden** was the **home of Adam and Eve**. It was the land where Adam and Eve lived.

Genesis 2:8

See also: Adam, Eve, Garden of Eden

Adam and Eve in Eden ➤

EDICT Daniel read the **edict** issued by the king. He read the **order the king gave to all the people**.

Daniel 6:7

EGYPT **Egypt** is a **country in Africa**.

The Nile River is part of Egypt. Long ago, God's people—the Israelites—lived in Egypt. The king of Egypt made the people slaves. Moses helped them escape. Jesus' parents took Him to Egypt when He was a baby. They were running from King Herod.

Exodus 1–3; Matthew 2:13–15

Ee

ELIHU   Elihu was **Job's friend**.

Elihu was upset with Job's friends
Eliphaz, Bildad, and Zophar. They said
God was mad at Job because Job did
many foolish things. But Job loved God.
He did nothing wrong. God was not mad at Job.

Job 32:1–5

ELIJAH   Elijah was a **prophet**.
He spoke God's words to the people.

He told the people they must stop
worshipping false gods.

1 Kings 18:16–39

ELIPHAZ   Eliphaz was **one of Job's friends**.

Many bad things happed to Job. Eliphaz tried
to make Job feel better by saying things that
sounded helpful and smart. But Eliphaz's words
were not God's words. So the things he said
only made Job feel worse!

Job 2:11, 4:1–21

Elisha – Emmanuel

ELISHA   **Elisha** was a **prophet of God**. He spoke God's words to the people of Israel. Elisha did amazing things in God's power. One of Elisha's miracles was bringing a dead boy back to life.

2 Kings 4:18–37

ELIZABETH   **Elizabeth** was Zacharias's wife and the **mother of John the Baptist**. She was also Mary's cousin.

Elizabeth knew Mary's baby was God's Son even before He was born!

Luke 1:39–45

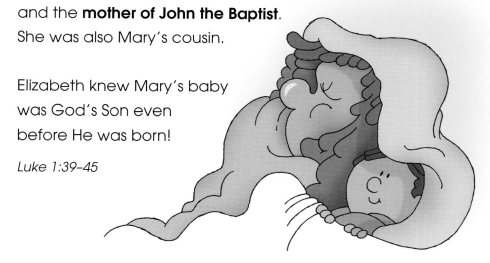

EMMANUEL   Isaiah said, "The Lord will give you a sign. The virgin will give birth to a son." "She will call him **Emmanuel**, which means **God with us**."

Jesus is our Emmanuel. He is God with us!

Isaiah 7:14

E

EMMAUS ROAD   Jesus showed himself to two of His disciples on the **Emmaus road**. He rose from the grave then walked on the **road between Jerusalem and the village of Emmaus.**

Luke 24:13–35

EMPTY TOMB   A **tomb** is a **place for a dead person**.

Jesus was in a tomb for three days. But when He came back to life, He left an empty tomb!

John 20:1–9

ENMITY   The LORD said, "I will put **enmity** between the serpent and the woman." They will **dislike each other very much.**

Genesis 3:15

ENOCH   Enoch was **Noah's great-grandfather**. He lived 365 years. His son Methuselah lived 969 years!

Enoch walked with God. He loved God and did what God said. Enoch **did not die**. God took him straight to heaven!

Genesis 5:21–27; Hebrews 11:5

Ephod – Esau

EPHOD   The high priest wore an **ephod**.

He wore a **beautiful, sleeveless garment made of linen**.

Exodus 28:6

A priest wearing an ephod ➤

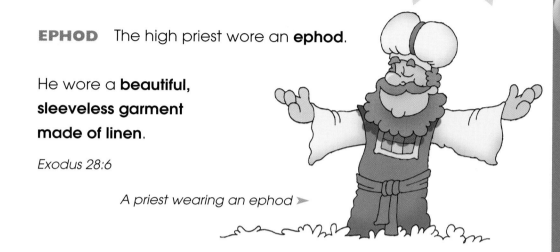

EPISTLE   An **epistle** is a **letter**. Many books of the Bible are letters to people and churches. Romans, Galatians, and 1 Timothy are all epistles.

Colossians 4:16

ESAU   **Esau** was the **firstborn of Isaac's twin sons**. Esau loved to hunt. He was covered with furry, red hair.

Esau let his brother Jacob trick him into selling his birthright for a bowl of stew.

Genesis 25:24–34

See also: Birthright

Ee

ESTHER   **Esther** was a Jewish girl who became the **queen of Persia**. She saved her people from the plans of an evil man named Haman.

Haman wanted king Xerxes to kill all the Jewish people. But Queen Esther helped the king to see it was wrong to kill them. So the king did not kill God's chosen people.

He killed Haman instead.

Esther 1–10

ETERNAL LIFE   Jesus went to the cross so we could have **eternal life**. He went to the cross so we could **live with God in heaven forever**!

John 3:16

EUTYCHUS   **Eutychus** was a man who **fell asleep during church**.

Eutychus fell asleep then fell out a window and died! The apostle Paul brought him back to life.

Acts 20:7–12

Evangelist – Evil Spirit

Go into all the world and preach the good news...

EVANGELIST Philip is an **evangelist**. He is a missionary who **tells people about God's love**.

Acts 21:8

EVE **Eve** was the **first woman**.

God made Eve from a rib taken from her husband Adam's side.

Genesis 2:21–22, 3:20

EVIL Turn away from **evil** and do good. Turn away from the **terrible, wicked things that cause others pain** and do good.

1 Peter 3:11

EVIL SPIRIT An **evil spirit** is a **helper of the devil**. Evil spirits caused trouble for people. Jesus made evil spirits leave people alone.

Luke 7:21

EWE   The little **ewe** slept softly in the shepherd's arms.

The little **female sheep** slept softly in his arms.

2 Samuel 12:3

EXILE   God's children were sent into **exile** in Babylon. They were taken from their homes and **forced to live in a faraway land**.

2 Kings 17:23

EXODUS   Moses and Aaron led the **Exodus** from Egypt. When Pharaoh said, "Go!" **all the people left at once**.

Exodus 12:31; Hebrews 11:22

EZEKIEL   **Ezekiel** was a **prophet of God**.

He spoke God's words to the people of Israel. The people were being punished in Babylon. Ezekiel told them God would make Israel strong again.

Ezekiel 1:2–3

Faith – False Prophet

FAITH **Faith** is being **sure of what we hope for**.
Faith is being certain of what we do not see.

By faith Abraham left his home and
headed for the Promised Land.

Abraham trusted God completely.
He did exactly what God said.

Hebrews 11

Abraham trusted God ➤

FAITHFUL God is **faithful**. We can trust Him.
He **always keeps His promises** no matter what.

Deuteronomy 7:9

FALSE PROPHET Hananiah was a **false prophet**.
He spoke lies that did not come from God.

Deuteronomy 18:22; Jeremiah 28; 1 John 4:1-3

Ff

FAMILY TREE   A **family tree** is a **list of a person's relatives** through time. It shows parents, grandparents, great-grandparents, and so on through history. Family trees were very important to the people of Israel.

Matthew 1:1

FAMINE   There was a **famine** in the land. The people had **no food to eat or water to drink**.

Genesis 12:10; Psalm 37:19

FAST   Sophie wanted to be closer to Jesus. She took time to **fast** and pray. She had a quiet time alone with God and **did not eat or drink** for a short time.

Isaiah 58:3–10; Matthew 6:16–18

FEASTS   The people of Israel celebrated many **feasts**. God's people celebrated many **holidays to remember special events in their history**.

Exodus 12:17

THE FEASTS OF THE BIBLE

Harvest, Ingathering, Lights, Tabernacles, Unleavened Bread, Weeks

Fellowship – Fiery Furnace

FELLOWSHIP   After church we will have a time of **fellowship**. We will have a **time of fun and friendship with people who love Jesus**.

Acts 2:42; 1 John 1:7

FESTIVAL   In the spring of each year, God's children would celebrate the **festival** of first fruits. His children had a **special time of worship, thanksgiving, and prayer**.

Exodus 23:14–16

See also: First Fruits

FIERY FURNACE   King Nebuchadnezzar threw Shadrach, Meshach, and Abednego into a **fiery furnace.** He was angry because they would not bow down and worship an idol.

The king threw them into a **big, hot oven made of stone**. But God protected them!

Daniel 3

FIG   A **fig** is the pear-shaped **fruit of a fig tree**.

Adam and Eve's first clothes were made of fig tree leaves.

Genesis 3:6–7

FIRE AND BRIMSTONE   God destroyed Sodom and Gomorrah with **fire and brimstone**. He made **hot burning sulfur** rain down from the sky.

Genesis 19:24

FIREBRAND   Samson tied **firebrands** to foxes' tails. He tied a small torch made from **pieces of burning wood** to their tails. When they ran off, they burned down the Philistines' fields.

Judges 15:3–5; Proverbs 26:18–19

FIRMAMENT   God said, "Let there be lights in the **firmament** of heaven." He said, "Let planets and stars fill the nighttime **sky**."

Genesis 1:14

72

Firstfruits – Fishers of Men

FIRSTFRUITS God asked for the **firstfruits** of His people's farms. God asked for the **first and best of their crops and animals**.

Exodus 23:19

FIRSTBORN Esau was Jacob's **firstborn** son. He was Jacob's oldest son. He was **the one born first**.

In Bible times, a firstborn son became leader of the family when his father died. He was given twice as many of his father's things as the other sons.

Genesis 27:19

FISHERS OF MEN Andrew and Peter were fishermen. They caught fish. But Jesus told them, "Come. Follow Me. I will make you **fishers of men**."

Now Andrew and Peter **tell everyone about God's love**. They fish people up from the water of sin and show them how to get to heaven.

Matthew 4:19

A B C D E **F** G H I J K L M N O P Q R S T U V W X Y Z

Ff

FLAMING SWORD   Angels guarded the path to the Tree of Life with **flaming swords**. Because Adam and Eve sinned, the path was protected by mighty angels. Their swords **blazed with fire but did not burn up**.

Genesis 3:24

FLAX   **Flax** is a **plant used to make cloth**. Two men who spied on Jericho hid under flax plants.

Joshua 2:1–6

FLEECE   Gideon placed a **fleece** on the threshing floor. He put down the **wooly covering of a sheep or goat**. Then he prayed and asked God to show him the right thing to do.

Judges 6:37

PUT OUT A FLEECE

Gideon had to make a big decision. He wanted to do the right thing. But he wasn't sure what to do. So before he did anything, Gideon did the best thing—he prayed and asked God to show him what to do.

Do you need to know the right thing to do? Jesus is ready to help you right now. No problem is too big or too small. All you have to do is ask.

Flog – Foal

FLOG The soldiers prepared to **flog** Jesus. They got ready to **hit him over and over again** with a whip, strap, or stick.

Mark 15:15

FLOOD, THE Because the people God made were sinful and would not change, God sent a great **flood** on the whole earth. He decided to make deep **water cover everyone and everything**.

Noah and his family were the only people who still loved God. So God decided to save them from the flood. He told Noah to build a huge boat. When the floodwater came, Noah, his family, and the animals on the ark were only living things in the whole world that did not die.

Genesis 6–8

See also: Noah, Noah's Ark

FOAL A **foal** is a **young horse or donkey**. Jesus rode a foal the last time He went to Jerusalem.

Matthew 21:1–9

FOOT WASHING   Jesus **showed His disciples how much He loved them** by washing their feet. He got down on His knees and did a dirty job with a humble heart.

Foot washing teaches us to let others **love and serve** us whether it makes us feel uncomfortable or not.

John 13:1–16

FORBIDDEN FRUIT   God told Adam and Eve not to eat the **forbidden fruit**. He told them not to eat the **fruit of the Tree of the Knowledge of Good and Evil**.

But Satan tricked them. When Adam and Eve ate the forbidden fruit, God had to send them out of the Garden of Eden, just like He said He would.

Genesis 2–3

FORGIVE   Jesus said, "**Forgive** and you will be forgiven." He said, "**Stop feeling hurt and angry** about the bad things others have done. Forget about their mistakes and I will forget about yours."

Luke 6:37

FORGIVEN   Jesus said, "Friend, your sins are **forgiven**."
He said, "Your **sins have been washed away** for ever and ever."

Luke 5:20

FORSAKE   God said, "I will never **forsake** you."
He said, "I will never **leave you or take My love away**."

Joshua 1:5

FRANKINCENSE   The wise men brought baby Jesus gold, **frankincense**, and myrrh.

They gave Jesus the **sweet-smelling sap of a beautiful tree**. The sap is thick like wax but smells like perfume.

Frankincense was burned as an offering of worship to God.

Matthew 2:11

See also: Gold, Myrrh

FRIEND OF GOD   Abraham **loved, trusted, and obeyed God.** He was the **friend of God!**

Genesis 15:6; Isaiah 41:8; James 2:23

FRUIT OF THE SPIRIT   The **fruit of the spirit** is a special name for the **good things God wants to grow in your life**.

There are nine kinds of fruit of the spirit: love, joy, peace, patience, kindness, goodness, faithfulness, gentleness, and self-control.

Galatians 5:22–23

Gg

G

GABRIEL Gabriel is an **angel**. He is God's messenger. Gabriel told Mary her baby would be Jesus, God's Son.

Luke 1:26–31

See also: Angel

GALILEE Jesus lived in **Galilee**. He lived in the **land of northern Israel** by the Sea of Galilee.

Jesus' boyhood home of Nazareth is in the land of Galilee.

Matthew 4:23

See also: Sea of Galilee

GALL **Gall** was used as a **medicine** to help people who were in pain. Gall was offered to Jesus when He was on the cross. But Jesus would not take it.

Matthew 27:34

A pot filled with gall ➤

GARDEN OF EDEN   God placed Adam in the **Garden of Eden** to care for it and work the soil.

He put Adam in a **beautiful garden**— a paradise filled with rivers and trees.

The Garden of Eden was Adam's and Eve's first home.

Adam gave the animals their names in the Garden of Eden.

Genesis 2:8–20

See also: Adam, Eve, Tree of the Knowledge of Good and Evil

GATH   Goliath came from the city of **Gath**.

He came from a **Philistine city in the land of Judah** west of the Dead Sea.

1 Samuel 17:4

See also: Dead Sea, Goliath, Judah

80

GAZELLE   A **gazelle** is a small **antelope**, like a deer, with long legs and curved horns.

The Bible says King David had soldiers who could run as fast as a wild **gazelle**.

1 Chronicles 12:8

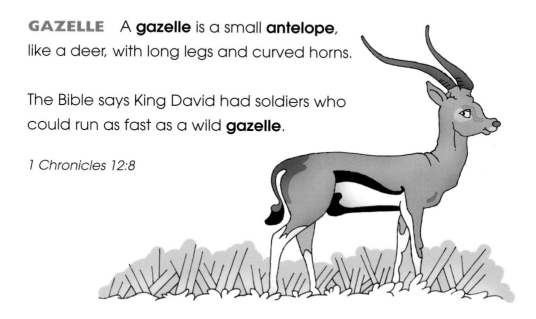

GEHAZI   **Gehazi** was a **helper of the prophet Elisha**.

Gehazi got in trouble after Elisha healed Naaman. Gehazi asked for Naaman's money. But he got Naaman's leprosy instead!

2 Kings 5

GENNESARET, LAKE   **Lake Genessaret** is another name for the **Sea of Galilee**. Jesus did many miracles near the Sea of Galilee.

Mark 1:16

See also: Galilee

GENTILE   Paul preached the Gospel to the **Gentiles**. He preached the good news about Jesus to the **people who were not Jewish**.

Acts 13:47

GERSHOM   **Gershom** and Eliezer were the sons of Moses and Zipporah. Gershom was **Moses' firstborn son**.

Exodus 2:21, 18:3–4

See also; Moses, Zipporah

GETHSEMANE   Jesus prayed in **Gethsemane** the night He was arrested.

Jesus prayed in **a garden near Jerusalem**.

Mark 14:32–46

Giant – Gideon's Army

GIANT   Goliath was a **giant**. He was **taller and stronger than everyone else** in the land.

Numbers 13:33; 1 Samuel 17:4

GIDEON   **Gideon** was the youngest, least important man from the weakest tribe in all Israel. But the Lord called him a **mighty warrior**. God said, "Go! I will be with you. You will strike down My enemies."

Gideon was afraid. But he trusted God and did what God said. So he struck down God's enemies just like God said he would!

Judges 6–7

See also: Fleece

GIDEON'S ARMY   **Gideon's army** saved Israel from the army of Midian. Gideon and **three hundred men** blew their trumpets, and God's enemies ran away without a fight.

Judges 7

Gg

GLEAN Ruth went out to **glean** in Boaz's field.

She **picked up leftover grain** the harvesters left behind to feed the poor.

Ruth 2:3

See also: Boaz, Naomi, Ruth

GLORY OF THE LORD The **glory of the LORD** shines where God meets with people. A **bright, fiery glow** shines where God meets with people.

Exodus 24:16–17

GLUTTON Porky the pot-bellied pig eats like a **glutton**.

He always **takes more food than he needs** and gulps it down as fast as he can.

Luke 7:34

Gnash – Goad

GNASH The religious leaders were furious and **gnashed** their teeth. They **ground their teeth together** in anger and rage.

Psalm 37:12

GNAT "Woe to you, teachers of the law and Pharisees!" Jesus said. "You strain out a **gnat** but swallow a camel."

A gnat is a **tiny two-winged insect** that bites like a mosquito.

Matthew 23:24

See also: Pharisee, Woe

GOAD A farmer uses a **goad** to guide his cows. The farmer uses a **sharp, pointed stick** to guide his cows.

Judges 3:31

Gg

GOBLET   King Solomon drank from a **goblet** made of pure gold.

He drank from a large **bowl-shaped cup** with a long stem and a round base.

1 Kings 10:21

GOD   There is only one **God**.

He is the **maker of all things**.
He has always been, and always will be, alive.
His love and kindness will never come to an end.
He is our heavenly Father, and He is our friend.

Isaiah 40:28–31; John 1:3–5; Revelation 1:8

GODLINESS   **Godliness** with contentment is great gain.

When you **live in a way that pleases God**, and are happy with what you have, you have a treasure no one can take away.

1 Timothy 6:6

Gold – Golgotha

GOLD   **Gold** is a **valuable metal**. People in Bible times used gold as money. Many of the things in God's temple were covered with gold.

Exodus 25

GOLDEN CALF   Aaron and the children of Israel made a **golden calf**.

They got tired of waiting for God to answer their prayers. So they made an **idol of gold** that looked like a cow. They prayed to that instead.

Exodus 32

See also: Idol

GOLGOTHA   Jesus was crucified at **Golgotha**. He was nailed to a cross on **a hill just outside the walls of Jerusalem**.

Golgotha means "the place of a skull."

Matthew 27:33

A B C D E F **G** H I J K L M N O P Q R S T U V W X Y Z

GOLIATH **Goliath** was a **Philistine giant**. He was the biggest, meanest man in the Philistine army.

Every man in the army of Israel was afraid to fight Goliath. But David was not afraid. He took on Goliath all by himself. Goliath was over nine feet tall. But David had a secret weapon. **David trusted God** with all his heart. Goliath never had a chance!

1 Samuel 17:4

GOOD NEWS "**Good news**" is the meaning of the word *Gospel*. Jesus preached good news to everyone. Jesus preached that people could be saved from their sins by believing in Him.

Mark 1:15

GOOD SAMARITAN The **Good Samaritan** put bandages on a man's wounds. The **man from Samaria** took care of the man and helped him feel better.

Davey is like the Good Samaritan. He is a very helpful young man.

Luke 10:30–37

GOPHER WOOD   Noah and his sons built the ark out of **gopher wood**.

They built the ark out of l**ong, strong timbers** covered with sticky, black tar.

Genesis 6:14

See also: Ark, Noah, Pitch

GOPHRITH   Noah covered the timbers of the ark with **gophrith**. He covered its timbers with **sticky, black tar** so the ark would not leak.

Genesis 6:14

GOSHEN   **Goshen** was an **area of Egypt**. Goshen was where Jacob and his family moved to escape a famine in Canaan.

Genesis 45:10

A B C D E F **G** H I J K L M N O P Q R S T U V W X Y Z

GOSPEL   Peter and John returned to Jerusalem and preached the **Gospel**. They told everyone in Jerusalem the **good news about Jesus**.

The Bible books Matthew, Mark, Luke, and John are called the Gospels. They tell about Jesus and the amazing things He said and did.

Mark 1:1; Acts 8:25

GOSSIP   "Without wood a fire goes out. Without **gossip** a quarrel dies down."

When we **say bad things about others** behind their back—especially when we don't know if those things are true— we are gossiping.

Proverbs 16:28, 26:20

GRACE   We have been saved by God's **grace**. Even though we don't deserve it, Jesus died to wash our sins away. It is God's **free gift** and can never be earned **by doing or being good**.

Ephesians 2:8

GRASSHOPPERS   **Grasshoppers** are big **green bugs** that love to eat plants.

Grasshoppers sometimes ate people's crops. But people could also eat the grasshoppers!

Psalm 78:46

GRAVEN IMAGE   God said, "You must not make any **graven images**. You must not bow down to them or worship them." He said, "Do not make **statues or pictures of false gods**. Do not bow down and worship them."

Exodus 20:4–5

GREED   Jezebel's heart was filled with **greed**. Her heart was filled with a **strong, selfish desire for money and power**.

Proverbs 15:27

GUILT   God forgave the **guilt** of my sin. **I had done wrong**, but God forgave me through Jesus.

Psalm 32:5

Hh

H

HABAKKUK **Habakkuk** was a **prophet of God**. He spoke God's words to the people in Judah. Habakkuk told the people why God would punish them. But he also thanked God for His salvation.

Habakkuk 1:1

HADES **Hades** is another name for **Hell**.

Jesus said, "On this rock I will build my church, and the gates of Hades will not have any power against it." Jesus said the gates of Hell will not have any power against God's children.

Matthew 16:18

HAGAR **Hagar** was an Egyptian servant of Abram and Sarai.

She was the **mother of Ishmael**.

Genesis 16:1

See also: Ishmael

Hailstones – Hallowed

HAILSTONES   Hailstones are **balls of ice and hardened snow** that sometimes fall from the sky during a thunderstorm.

Hailstones were one of the ten plagues God sent on Egypt because Pharaoh would not let God's people go.

Exodus 9:22

See also: Plague

HALLELUJAH   People shout "**Hallelujah!**" when they worship God. People are shouting "**Praise the Lord!**"

Revelation 19:1

HALLOWED   God's name is **hallowed**. His name is **holy**.

Matthew 6:9

See also: Holy

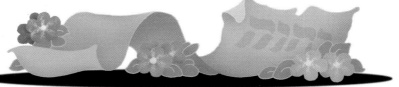

Hh

HAM   **Ham** was **one of Noah's sons**. He and his brothers Shem and Japheth helped Noah build the ark.

Genesis 6:10

HAMAN   **Haman** was the **king of Persia's powerful official**. He wanted the king to kill all the Jewish people.

But Queen Esther convinced the king it was wrong to kill the Jewish people. So the king did not kill them.

He killed Haman instead!

Esther 3:1

See also: Esther, Mordecai, Xerxes

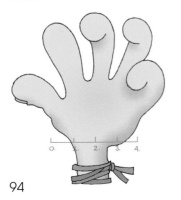

HANDBREADTH   A **handbreadth** is a type of **measurement**. In Bible times, people used their hands to measure. A handbreadth is about four inches.

Exodus 37:12

Hannah – Harp

HANNAH **Hannah** was the **mother of Samuel.**

Hannah was very sad. She thought she would never have a baby. But the Lord answered her prayer and gave her a strong, beautiful son.

1 Samuel 1

HARDENED HEART Haman has a **hardened heart.** He **does not care about God**. A person with a hardened heart does not trust God, believe God, or want to hear anything God has to say.

2 Chronicles 36:13

HARP A **harp** is a **musical instrument** with strings stretched across a triangular frame. It is played by plucking.

David wrote beautiful songs of worship and praise on the harp.

1 Chronicles 15:16; Psalm 98:5

HARVEST   A farmer works to collect a **harvest**.
The farmer works to collect **more of what he planted**. Jesus
said that He worked to collect a harvest of people's souls.

Matthew 9:37–38

HAUGHTY   Hamor has a **haughty** heart. His heart is **proud**.
He thinks and acts like he is better than everyone else.

Proverbs 16:18

HEALED   The blind and lame came to Jesus and He
healed them. He touched the people who were sick
and they were **made well**.

Matthew 21:14

See also: Blind, Lame

HEART   Danielle loves Jesus with all of her **heart**.
She loves Jesus deep down inside with her **truest,
strongest feelings**.

Deuteronomy 6:5; Matthew 5:8; Romans 10:8

Heathen – Heaven

HEATHEN   The **heathen** are **people who are not Jewish.**
The heathen are people who are not God's chosen people,
the Israelites.

Ezekiel 22:15

HEAVEN   **Heaven** is **God's home.**

Jesus said, "There are many rooms in my Father's house.
I am going there now to get a room ready just for you!"

Psalm 115:15, 136:26; John 14:1-4; Philippians 2:10

ONE SMALL STEP

Jesus loves you so much He stepped out of heaven.

It's true. He stepped out of heaven and stepped into
a human body!

He gave up being like God to become like you and
me. And because He did, one day we will step out
of our bodies, and step into heaven with Him.

HEAVENLY FATHER   **God** is our **heavenly Father**. He loves us. He made us. He gave us life. When we love Him and put Him first, we will always have everything we need.

Matthew 6:25–26

HEAVENS   The **heavens** declare the glory of God!

"The heavens" are what you see when you look up in **the sky**. The stars and planets, and all the beautiful, mysterious things in it—both near and far—make up the **heavens**.

Genesis 1:1; Psalm 19:1

HEBREW   *Hebrew* is a **name for God's special people**, the people of Israel. "Hebrew" is also the name of the language the Israelites spoke.

Genesis 14:13; Luke 23:38

Heifer – Hell

HEIFER A **heifer** is a young **female cow** that has not yet had a baby.

1 Samuel 16:2

A red heifer ➤

HELL Hell is the **place where Satan lives.**

If a person will not give their heart to Jesus, one day they will find themselves in hell. It is a terrible place, like a lake filled with fire, cut off from God forever and ever.

Luke 12:5; John 3:16; 2 Thessalonians 1:9; Revelation 19:20

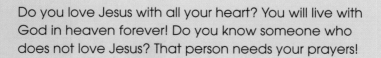

THEY NEED TO KNOW!

Do you love Jesus with all your heart? You will live with God in heaven forever! Do you know someone who does not love Jesus? That person needs your prayers!

They need to know about God's love and the good things He can do—today!

Hh

HELPMEET   Eve was Adam's "**helpmeet.**"
Eve was Adam's **helper and mate**.

Genesis 2:18

HERALD   A **herald** is a **messenger** sent to bring important
news. A herald would stand in the street and give his message
in a loud voice so everyone could hear.

Habakkuk 2:2

HERD   A **herd** of brown cows fed happily on the hillside.
A **large group** of cows fed happily on the hills.

Jeremiah 31:12

Herod – Holiness

HEROD   **Herod the Great** was the **king of Israel** when Jesus was born. Herod heard the Messiah had been born in Bethlehem. He was afraid this Messiah would grow up to be king. So he had every boy under two years old killed. Mary and Joseph ran away to Egypt to save baby Jesus' life.

Herod the Great had a son named **Herod Antipas**. Herod Antipas was the **ruler of Galilee** when Jesus was crucified. Herod Antipas put John the Baptist to death. Pontius Pilate sent Jesus to Herod Antipas. He mocked Jesus and sent Him back to Pilate be crucified.

Matthew 2:16; Luke 23:6–12

HIGH PRIEST   Aaron was the first **high priest** of Israel. Aaron was the first **leader of the priests**. Priests helped people worship God. Jesus is now our "great high priest."

Exodus 28; Hebrews 4:15

HOLINESS   Like the light and warmth that shine from the sun, **holiness** is the **power and beauty of who God is**. It is also the way Jesus wants us to live—giving our hearts, our minds, our hands, and our feet to God. Then He can use them any way His heart desires.

Psalm 96:9; Ephesians 4:24; 1 Timothy 2:2

HOLY   Holy means **belonging to God, coming from God**, or **set apart for God to use**.

Genesis 2:3; Deuteronomy 7:6; Ephesians 1:4

HOLY GROUND   God called to Moses from inside the burning bush. "Take off your sandals," God said, "the place you are standing is **holy ground**."

The place where Moses stood was **filled with God's beauty, power and love**.

Exodus 3:5

HOLY OF HOLIES   The **holy of holies** was a special room in the tabernacle and temple. The holy of holies was the **place God would meet with the high priest**. The ark of the covenant was kept in the holy of holies.

Hebrews 9:1–7

Holy Spirit – Horns of the Altar

HOLY SPIRIT   God is like three persons wrapped up in one. He is God the Father, God the Son, and God the **Holy Spirit**.

The Holy Spirit is **our helper**. He helps us understand God's Word. He helps us know when we do wrong. He comforts us when we are worried or afraid. He **fills us with power, faith, and love** so we can be all God wants us to be.

John 14:15–17; Acts 1:8, 2:4

HOPE   **Hope** is trusting God no matter what. Hope is **knowing the good things you look forward to are going to happen.**

Hebrews 11:1

HORNS OF THE ALTAR   Adonijah took hold of the **horns of the altar.** He held on to the **triangular posts on the four corners of the altar.**

1 Kings 1:50

See also: Altar

◄ The horns of the altar

A
B
C
D
E
F
G
H
I
J
K
L
M
N
O
P
Q
R
S
T
U
V
W
X
Y
Z

A B C D E F G **H** I J K L M N O P Q R S T U V W X Y Z

HOSANNA   People shouted "**Hosanna**!" to Jesus.
People were shouting "**Jesus, save us now**!"

Matthew 21:9

HUMILITY   Hana serves with **humility**. She is modest and respectful and **does not think she is more important** than everyone else.

Proverbs 11:2; Philippians 2:3

HUSBANDMAN   Like a **farmer** or a gardener, a **husbandman** prepares the soil for planting. He works the land with patience and love to make sure his plants grow tall and strong.

John 15:1

Hymns – Hyssop

HYMNS   Paul and Silas sang **hymns** and prayed. They sang beautiful **songs of worship and praise** to God.

Acts 16:25

HYPOCRITE   A **hypocrite** is a person who **says one thing but does another**. Jesus was very angry with hypocrites.

Matthew 23:13–14

HYSSOP   Hyssop is a **small, bushy plant** with sweet-smelling blue flowers.

Exodus 12:22; Psalm 51:7

See also: Passover

A hyssop bush in bloom ➤

I AM – Image of God

I **I AM** When the Children of Israel wanted to know **God's name**, God told Moses to tell them, "My name is **I AM**." He said, "I Am God. I Am alive!" "I Am the One who made all things. I Am the One who gives you life.

I have always been—and will always be—the One True God."

Exodus 3:14; John 8:58

IDOL An **idol** is a **man-made, pretend god** that people worship instead of the One True God.

Exodus 20:4; Leviticus 26:1; Jonah 2:8

STONE COLD

When you pray to an idol and trust it for help, you trade all the good things God wants to pour into your heart for a pile of cold, hard, lifeless stone.

IMAGE OF GOD People were made in the **image of God**. People were **made to think and act like God**. Because of sin, people don't think and act like God. But Jesus can bring us back into the image of God.

Genesis 1:27; Colossians 1:15–20

INCENSE **Incense** is a **gum, spice, or powder** burned for the sweet smelling smoke it makes. In Bible times the priest burned incense on the altar as a part of worship.

Exodus 30:34–36; Leviticus 2:2; Psalm 141:2

INHERITANCE When Abraham dies, Isaac will receive an **inheritance**. Isaac will become the owner of his **father's money, land, and things** when Abraham passes away.

Exodus 32:13

INN An **inn** is a **place where travelers can rest**. Jesus was born in a manger because there was no room in the inn.

Luke 2:6–7

See also: Manger

107

INSPIRATION God used **inspiration** to make the Bible. God **breathed out His words** to Bible writers.

2 Timothy 3:16

INTERCESSION Paul made **intercession** for Timothy. Paul **prayed over and over again** for his friend Timothy.

1 Timothy 2:1

Paul prayed for Timothy ➤

ISAAC Isaac was **Abraham and Sarah's son.** Abraham was 100 years old when Isaac was born.

Isaac's name means "laughter."

Abraham and Sarah named their son Isaac because Sarah laughed with joy when she found out she would have a child in her old age.

Genesis 21:1–7

See also: Abraham, Sarah

108

Isaiah – Israel

ISAIAH Isaiah was a **prophet** in Old Testament times. He spoke God's words to the people. Isaiah gave people the good news that a Savior would be born. He gave them this news about 700 years before it happened!

Isaiah 7:14, 9:6

ISHMAEL Ishmael was **Abraham's oldest son**. But Abraham didn't have Ishmael with his wife, Sarah. He had Ishmael with Sarah's servant girl, Hagar. Abraham and Sarah should have trusted God's promise that they would have a baby together. They did have a baby—Isaac—fourteen years later.

Genesis 16

ISRAEL The land of **Israel** is the **home of the Jewish people**. It is the new name God gave Jacob after Jacob wrestled with an angel.

The Twelve Tribes—Jacob's twelve sons, their families, and all of their children and children's children—came to be known as the "nation of Israel."

Genesis 32:28; 2 Chronicles 1:13; Psalm 106:48; Romans 11:26

See also: Jacob, Jews, Twelve Tribes of Israel

J

JACOB **Jacob** was the **second of Isaac's twin sons**. Jacob tricked his brother Esau into selling his birthright for a bowl of stew. Esau became very angry. So Jacob ran away! They did not see each other for many years.

When Jacob was older, he wrestled with an angel. "I won't let you go unless you bless me!" Jacob told the angel. So the angel blessed Jacob with a new name. Jacob's name became Israel.

Genesis 25:24–34, 32:22–31

JACOB'S LADDER **One night Jacob had a dream**. He saw a ladder, like a **stairway that went all the way to heaven**. Angels walked up and down on **Jacob's ladder**.

At the top was God. He promised Jacob all the people on earth will be blessed because of him.

Genesis 28:10–15

JAIRUS'S DAUGHTER **Jairus's daughter** was a **girl Jesus brought back to life**. She was twelve years old when she died. But Jesus touched her hand and told her to get up. And she did!

Luke 8:49–56

James – Javelin

JAMES **James** was **one of Jesus' disciples**. James and his brother John were known as the Sons of Thunder.

Matthew 4:21; Mark 3:17

JAPHETH **Japheth** was **one of Noah's sons**. He was born when Noah was 500 years old!

Japheth helped Noah build the ark.

Genesis 5:32, 7:13

JAVELIN Goliath had a bronze **javelin** slung across his back. He carried a **long, thin spear**. It was light and could be thrown a long way.

1 Samuel 17:6

Jj

Jehoshaphat – Jehovah-Nissi

JEHOSHAPHAT Jehoshaphat was a **king of Judah**. He led God's people from Jerusalem.

Jehoshaphat was a good king who helped his people learn about God. But he made a mistake when he became friends with evil King Ahaziah of Israel.

2 Chronicles 17, 20

JEHOVAH Jehovah is an ancient, Holy **name for God**.

Exodus 6:3; Revelation 19:11–16

JEHOVAH-JIREH Jehovah-Jireh means **God is my provider**. He will give us everything we need.

Genesis 22:14

JEHOVAH-NISSI Jehovah-Nissi means **God is my banner**. He will help us fight our battles.

Exodus 17:15

112

Jehovah-Shalom – Jericho

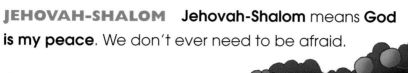

JEHOVAH-SHALOM Jehovah-Shalom means **God is my peace**. We don't ever need to be afraid.

Judges 6:24

JEREMIAH **Jeremiah** was a **prophet**. He spoke God's words to the people. Jeremiah told the people to turn away from their sins. God picked Jeremiah to speak His words before he was even born!

Jeremiah 1, 29:11–13

JERICHO For seven days Joshua and his army marched around **Jericho**. They marched around a **walled city near the Jordan River and the Dead Sea**.

When the priests blew their trumpets, God's people shouted, and the walls of Jericho came tumbling down.

Joshua 6:1–20

A B C D E F G H I **J** K L M N O P Q R S T U V W X Y Z

JERUSALEM Jesus went up to **Jerusalem**. He rode into the **Holy city of God's chosen people** on the back of a donkey. Jerusalem is a very old city. Many special things happened in Jerusalem.

Abraham lived near Jerusalem. King David brought the ark that held the Ten Commandments into Jerusalem. King Solomon built God's temple in Jerusalem. God made the sun stand still for Joshua over Jerusalem. Jesus was crucified on a hill just outside the city wall of Jerusalem.

Joshua 10:12–13; 2 Samuel 6:12; 1 Kings 8:1–11; Matthew 21:10

JESUS **Jesus** is the **Son of God**. He is the savior of the world.

Jesus was born as a baby in Bethlehem two thousand years ago. But He lived with God forever before that. Jesus died on a cross to take the punishment for our sins. He wants to forgive us for the wrong things we do.

Jesus came back to life three days after He died. Today, He lives in heaven. Someday, He will come back to take His followers to heaven with Him!

Matthew 1:18–23; John 1:1; Luke 24:1–6; 1 Thessalonians 4:16–17

JEWS   God's chosen people—**the children of Israel**—are known as the **Jews**. *Hebrews, Israelites,* and *the Jewish people* are also names for the Jews.

Matthew 2:2; John 19:19; Romans 3:29

JEZEBEL   **Jezebel** was the **wife of king Ahab**. She was a very, very naughty queen. Jezebel killed God's prophets. She forced God's children to worship Baal. She even killed an innocent man so the king could take away his land.

1 Kings 16:31, 21:1–16

JOB   **Job** was a very **good man who had very bad things happen** to him. Job loved God. And God loved him.

Satan wanted to see if Job would turn his back on God. He made many bad things happen to Job. But Job did not turn his back on God.

So God did not turn His back on Job. He gave back everything the devil tried to take away.

Job 1–42

JOCHEBED **Jochebed** was the **mother of Moses,** Aaron, and Miriam. Jochebed saved Moses' life when the king of Egypt wanted to kill the baby boys of Israel. She put Moses in a basket in the river. The king's daughter found Moses and raised him as her own son.

Numbers 26:59

JOEL **Joel** was a **prophet**. He spoke God's words to the people. He begged them to turn away from sin and give their hearts to God. He told them about the Holy Spirit and the healing He can bring. He let them know that everyone who calls on the LORD will be saved.

Joel 2:12–13, 28, 32

JOHN **John** was **one of the twelve apostles.**

He was Jesus' disciple and close friend. John called himself the disciple Jesus loved. John wrote down everything he saw Jesus say and do in the Gospel of John.

John 13:23

John the Baptist – Jonathan

JOHN THE BAPTIST   **John the Baptist** was a prophet. He **led many people to Jesus**. John told everyone to prepare their  hearts for the coming of God's Son. He wore clothes made of camel hair. He ate locusts and wild honey. John preached in the desert and baptized many people. He even baptized Jesus!

Isaiah 40:3; John 1:23

JONAH   **Jonah** was a **prophet**. God asked him to tell a whole city full of very naughty people they needed to change.

But Jonah was afraid. He tried to run away from God. So God had a huge fish swallow Jonah and spit him out in the place God told him to go!

Jonah 1–4

JONATHAN   **Jonathan** was the **son of king Saul**. He was David's best friend. King Saul was jealous of David for killing Goliath. Saul told Jonathan to kill David. But Jonathan would not. He helped David get away instead.

1 Samuel 18:1–3, 19:1, 2:1–42

JORDAN RIVER Jesus was baptized in the **Jordan River**. He was baptized in the **river that flows from the Sea of Galilee to the Dead Sea**.

Matthew 3:13

JOSEPH **Joseph** was **Jacob's favorite son**.

Jacob gave Joseph a coat of many colors. Joseph's brothers were jealous of his beautiful coat. They threw him into a well and sold him as a slave! But Joseph did not get angry at his brothers. He forgave them! Joseph grew up to be a powerful man and helped his brothers when they needed him most.

Joseph was also the name of **Mary's husband**. He was Jesus' earthly father.

Genesis 37:3; Matthew 1:20

JOSHUA **Joshua** was a **leader of God's people**. Joshua led the people after Moses died. Joshua was a brave soldier who led the people into the Promised Land.

Joshua 1:1–3

Joy – Judah

JOY   Mary's heart was filled with **joy**.

She had **happiness and thankfulness** deep down in her heart.

Luke 2:10

JUBILEE   The fiftieth year will be a year of **Jubilee**. It will be **a time to celebrate** all the good things God has done.

Leviticus 25:8–12

JUDAH   **Judah** was **one of Jacob's sons**.

It is also the name of one of the Twelve Tribes of Israel. Jesus was known as the Lion of the tribe of Judah.

Exodus 1:1–5; Revelation 5:5

Left margin: A B C D E F G H I **J** K L M N O P Q R S T U V W X Y Z

Jj

JUDAS   Judas was a **popular name in Jesus' time**.

Jesus had two disciples named Judas. Jesus also had a brother named Judas.

Matthew 13:55

JUDAS ISCARIOT   Judas Iscariot was the **disciple who betrayed Jesus**.

He told Jesus' enemies where to find Him so Jesus could be captured, beaten, and killed.

John 13:2

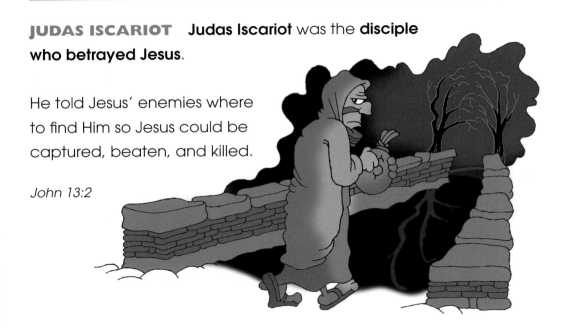

JUDEA   Pontius Pilate was the governor of **Judea**. He ruled the **land in southern Israel that included Bethlehem and Jerusalem**.

Luke 3:1–3

See also: Israel, Pilate

120

Judges – Judgement

JUDGES   In the time of the **judges**, Israel had no king. Everyone did whatever seemed right in their own eyes.

The people forgot about God. They began to worship idols. Their enemies attacked. They cried out to God for help. So God sent them a judge. He sent a **person to lead the army**.

Things got better for awhile. . .

But soon the people forgot about God. They began to worship idols. They cried out to God for help. So God sent them a person to lead the army. . .

and it started all over again!

Judges 21:25

Right   Wrong   Whatever

JUDGMENT   **Judgment** is God's **punishment for sin**. God has to punish the wrong things people do. But Jesus took that punishment for everyone when He died on the cross!

Romans 5:15–17

ABCDEFGHIJK K LMNOPQRSTUVWXYZ

Kk

KID Sophie fed her **kids** beside the shepherd's tents. She fed her **baby goats** beside the shepherd's tents.

Luke 15:29

KINDRED "Isn't Boaz one of our **kindred**?" Naomi asked Ruth. "Isn't he **one of our relatives**—a member of our family?"

Ruth 3:2

KING David was the **king** of Israel.

He was the **man who ruled the people** of Israel.

2 Samuel 5:4

King Herod – King of the Jews

KING HEROD **King Herod** was the **ruler of Judea when Jesus was born**.

The wise men told Herod they were looking for a king who had just been born.

Herod didn't want another king to take his place. So he tried to kill all the young boys in the land. God protected Jesus by sending His family to Egypt.

Matthew 2:1–16

KING OF KINGS Jesus is the **King of kings**. He is **the One who rules over every other king** everywhere.

Revelation 19:16

See also: Lord of Lords

KING OF THE JEWS Jesus is the **King of the Jews**. He is the **messiah**—the promised ruler of the Hebrew people.

John 19:19

See also: Messiah

123

Kk

Kingdom – Kinsman Redeemer

KINGDOM   A **kingdom** is the **land ruled by a king**.

1 Chronicles 14:2

KINGDOM OF GOD   The **kingdom of God** is a **place in the heart of Jesus' followers**. When you believe Jesus and let God rule your life, the kingdom of God is inside you!

Luke 17:20–21

KINSMAN-REDEEMER   Boaz is Ruth's **kinsman-redeemer**.

He is the person in her family who **pays a debt she could not pay**.

Jesus' death on the cross paid the price to take away our sins.

Jesus is our kinsman-redeemer.

▲ *Ruth and Boaz*

Ruth 3:9

Laban – Lamb

LABAN   **Laban** was **Jacob's uncle**. Rebekah sent Jacob to Laban's house to hide him from Esau.

Jacob fell in love with Laban's daughter Rachel. He worked for seven years to make her his wife.

But Laban tricked Jacob into marrying his other daughter Leah. Jacob worked for Laban seven more years to marry Rachel.

Genesis 29:15–30

LAKE OF FIRE   The devil, the beast, and the false prophet were thrown into the **Lake of Fire**. The Lake of Fire is another name for **hell**.

Revelation 20:10

LAMB   A **lamb** is a **young sheep**.

Lambs were used for food and clothing. Lambs were also used as sacrifices. They were given to God to pay for sins.

Genesis 22:6–8

A B C D E F G H I J K L M N O P Q R S T U V W X Y Z

LAMB OF GOD   Jesus is the **Lamb of God**. He is the sacrifice whose blood **takes away the sins of the world**.

John 1:29

See also: Sacrifice, Sin

LAME   Jesus healed the little girl who was **lame**. He healed the girl who **could not walk normally** because she was hurt or sick.

Matthew 21:14

LAST SUPPER   Jesus' **final Passover meal** was called the **Last Supper**. It was the last meal Jesus shared with the disciples before He was crucified.

Luke 22:14–22

See also: Passover

Peter and Jesus eating the Last Supper ▲

Laver – Laying on of Hands

LAVER   In the Tabernacle, God's priests would wash their hands and feet in a bronze **laver**. The priests would wash in a **metal container full of water**.

Exodus 30:17–21

The laver ➤

LAW OF MOSES   The rules God gave to the children of Israel in the **first five books of the Bible** are called the **Law of Moses**. The Law of Moses helped God's children know right from wrong.

Deuteronomy 5:1; Luke 24:44

LAYING ON OF HANDS   Jacob **laid his hands on** Ephraim and Manasseh. He touched their heads with his hands and **asked God to bless them**.

Genesis 48:17–20

LAZARUS   **Lazarus** was the **brother of Mary and Martha**. Mary and Martha were very sad when Lazarus died. Jesus was very sad, too. So Jesus told the two sisters to take away the stone that covered Lazarus' grave. Then Jesus raised Lazarus from the dead!

John 11:1–44

See also: Mary and Martha, Miracle

LEAH   **Leah** was a **wife of Jacob**. Leah was the older sister of Rachel. Jacob loved Rachel, but was tricked into marrying Leah first. Leah and Jacob had six sons together. They were leaders of the twelve tribes of Israel.

Genesis 29:16–30

LEAVEN   **Leaven** is the yeast that **makes a loaf of bread rise**.

Paul said, "Don't you know that a little leaven leavens the whole lump?" He told us it only takes a little bit of sin to make all of God's children sick at heart.

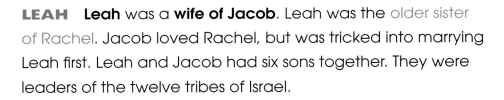

1 Corinthians 5:6

128

Leek – Leviathan

LEEK A **leek** is like an **onion** with a long bulb and large, flat green leaves. The Israelites liked to eat onions and leeks.

Numbers 11:5

LEGION A **legion** is a very **large number of people or things**. Jesus said, "Don't you know I can ask my Father to send twelve legions of angels to protect us and He will send them right away?"

Matthew 26:53

LEVIATHAN The **leviathan** was a **powerful creature** with sharp teeth that lived in the water.

It may have been something like a crocodile—or even a dinosaur!

Job 41; Psalm 104:26; Isaiah 27:1

129

LEVITES Moses and Aaron were **Levites**. They **were members of the tribe of Levi**. The Levites took care of the Tabernacle and the temple.

Numbers 1:50, 26:59

LICE **Lice** are **small, wingless insects** that live on the skin. Lice were one of the ten plagues God sent on Egypt because Pharaoh would not let God's people go.

Exodus 8:16–17

LIGHT **Light** is the **power that makes darkness go away**. Light was one of the first things God created. Light is what makes day different from night. Jesus said He is the "light of the world." He helps people "see" through the "darkness" of sin.

Genesis 1:3; John 9:5

Light of Life – Linen

LIGHT OF LIFE **Jesus** is the **light of life**. He shows us the way God wants us to live.

John 8:12

LIGHT OF THE WORLD **Jesus** is the **light of the world**. When we follow Him, we will never lose our way.

John 8:12

LET THERE BE LIGHT!

Jesus said, "I am the light of the world. Whoever follows me will never walk in darkness, but have the light of life." John 8:12

In Jesus was life, and that life was the light of men. The light shines in the darkness, but the darkness has not understood it. John 1:4–5

God's word is a lamp unto my feet, and a light unto my path. Psalm 119:105

LINEN Pharaoh dressed Joseph in robes of fine **linen**. He wore beautiful robes made from the **fibers of spun flax**. Like cotton, flax is a plant whose fibers can be used to make clothing.

Genesis 41:42

A B C D E F G H I J K L M N O P Q R S T U V W X Y Z

LION A **lion** is a **large, dangerous, wild cat**. Daniel was punished by being thrown into a den of lions. But God protected him.

Daniel 6:1–24

LION OF JUDAH **Jesus** is the **Lion of Judah**. He is the mighty King of all men and the ruler of all things both now and forever.

Revelation 5:5; Genesis 49:9–10

LION'S DEN A **den** is a **place where wild animals make their home**. King Darius threw Daniel into the lion's den.

Daniel 6:1–24

id="1"

Living God – Loaves and Fishes

LIVING GOD The people turned from their idols and began to worship the **living God**. They began to worship **Jesus**—the One True God—maker of heaven and earth.

Acts 14:15

LIVING WATER **Living water** is the power of **God's Holy Spirit** flowing in, out, and through a believer's life. Jesus promised living water to anyone who would ask.

John 7:37–39

LOAVES AND FISHES Jesus fed five thousand with the **loaves and fishes**. He fed five thousand people with **five pieces of bread and two little fishes**.

John 6:1–14

LOCUST   **Locusts** are **large, hungry insects** that fly in huge swarms. Locusts cause great damage by eating all the crops they find in their path.

Exodus 10:12

See also: Plague

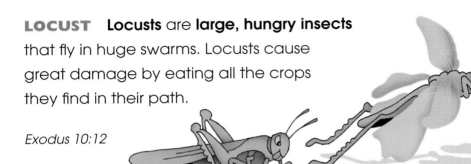

LONGSUFFERING   Anna endured the other children's insults with gentleness and **longsuffering**. She showed **patience** with her friends. She did her best to put up with their faults without anger, bitterness, or trying to hurt them back.

Ephesians 4:2

LORD   **Lord** is a word for a **very important person**. Sometimes in the Bible, kings are called "lord." But with a capital "L", God and Jesus are called Lord.

Genesis 2:4; Acts 16:31

LORD OF LORDS   **Jesus** is the **Lord of Lords**. He is the One True King who rules over every king everywhere.

Revelation 19:16

Lord's Day – Lord's Prayer

LORD'S DAY   **Sunday** is the **Lord's Day**. It is the special day when we set aside our work and gather together with other believers to worship God.

Exodus 20:8–11; Revelation 1:10

LORD'S PRAYER   The **Lord's Prayer** are special Bible verses Jesus gave us to **teach us how to pray**. More than just a list to repeat or remember, the Lord's Prayer reminds us to think about all the good things God has done for us when we bow our hearts to pray.

Matthew 6:9–13

THE LORD'S PRAYER

"When you pray, you should pray like this: 'Our Father in heaven, may your name always be kept holy. May your kingdom come and what you want be done, here on earth as it is in heaven.

Give us the food we need for each day. Forgive us for our sins, just as we have forgiven those who sinned against us. And do not cause us to be tempted, but save us from the Evil One.'"

Matthew 6:9–13 NCV

A B C D E F G H I J K L M N O P Q R S T U V W X Y Z

LORD'S SUPPER   The **Lord's supper** was **Jesus' final meal with His disciples**. Jesus told His followers to eat and drink and remember His death for sins. Many Christians call the Lord's supper "communion."

Matthew 26:26–28

LOT   Lot was **Abraham's nephew**. He lived in the city of **Sodom**.

The people of Sodom were very naughty. So God decided to destroy the city. An angel told Lot and his family to run away and never look back. Lot and his daughters did as they were told. But Lot's wife looked back and was turned into a pillar of salt!

Genesis 19:1–26

LOTS   The Roman soldiers cast **lots** to decide who would get Jesus' robes. They made a choice by **throwing dice, flipping a coin, or drawing straws**.

Mark 15:24

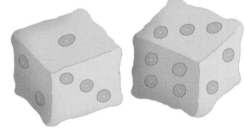

A pair of Roman dice ➤

Lotus – Lucifer

LOTUS   A **lotus** is a large **plant,** like a **water lily, with beautiful white or pink flowers.**

Job 40:21

LOVE   **Love** is true **concern for other people.**

Love can be a strong like for someone else. Or love can be a choice to care for their needs. God loved the world so much He sent Jesus to die for sins. God's people are to love Him and each other.

Matthew 22:37–40; John 3:16

LUCIFER   **Lucifer** is a **very old name** people often used for **Satan.** Satan is another name for the devil.

Isaiah 14:12

See also: Satan

LUKE **Luke** was a **doctor who wrote** about all the things Jesus said and did. Luke was a good friend of the apostle Paul. He examined the facts about Jesus and His followers and wrote them down with great care. Luke shared the things he learned in the book of Acts and the Gospel of Luke.

Luke; Acts

LUKEWARM David's meal is **lukewarm**. It is **neither hot nor cold**.

Revelation 3:16

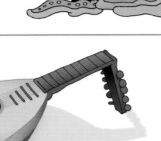

LUTE A **lute** is a **musical instrument like a guitar**. People in Bible times used the lute to praise God.

2 Chronicles 20:27–28

LYRE Lydia loves to play the **lyre**. She loves to play a **little U-shaped harp** she can hold in her hands.

Psalm 144:9

Magdala – Magician

MAGDALA Mary lived in **Magdala**. She lived in a **village on the shore of the Sea of Galilee**.

Matthew 15:39; Mark 16:9

MAGI **Magi** are **wise men**.

When Jesus was born, magi came from the east to visit Him. They brought gifts of gold, frankincense, and myrrh for Jesus and His parents.

Matthew 2:1-12

MAGICIAN The king called for his **magicians**, but they were not able to help him. He called for the **people who use the devil's power** to hurt others, do tricks that fill people's hearts with fear, or learn about things to come.

God's word tells us to stay far away from magic and sorcery.

Leviticus 19:26; Ezekiel 13:20; Daniel 2:27; Revelation 21:8

A B C D E F G H I J K L **M** N O P Q R S T U V W X Y Z

Majesty – Manger

MAJESTY The Lord is robed with **majesty**. He is clothed with **power, beauty, kindness, and love**.

Psalm 93:1, 145:5; Jude 24–25

MAMMON You cannot serve God and **mammon**. You cannot serve God if what your heart really wants is **money, money, money**.

Luke 16:13

MANGER A **manger** is a **wooden box that holds food for an animal**. When Jesus was born, His mother laid Him in a manger.

Luke 2:7

MANNA   "What is it?" the children of Israel asked as tiny white flakes fell from the sky.

It is **manna**—sweet, white **bread that fell from heaven** to feed God's people.

Exodus 16:14–16

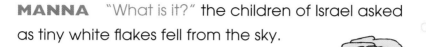

MARANATHA

Paul said, "**Maranatha**!" He said, "**Come, Lord Jesus**!"

1 Corinthians 16:22

MARK   **Mark** was the cousin of Barnabas.

He went with Barnabas and Paul on their first missionary journey. Mark was the **first person to write down the good news about Jesus**. He wrote about all the good things Jesus said and did in the Gospel of Mark.

Acts 12:25; Colossians 4:10

See also: Barnabas, Gospel, Paul

MARTHA AND MARY **Martha and Mary** were **close friends of Jesus**. They were sisters from a town called Bethany, with a brother named Lazarus. One time, Jesus came to their home. Martha complained that she was doing all the work while Mary just visited with Jesus. Jesus said Mary was doing the right thing.

Luke 10:38–42

MARY **Mary** was **Jesus' mother**.

She was married to Joseph.
An angel told Mary she would
give birth to the Son of God.

Matthew 1:18; Luke 1:46–55

See also: Joseph

MARY MAGDALENE **Mary Magdalene** was the **first to tell the disciples Jesus had risen from the dead**. She saw Jesus alive three days after He was crucified and buried. Mary talked with Jesus, then ran off to tell the disciples the good news!

John 20:10–18

Mat – Matthias

MAT "Get up!" Jesus told the crippled man. "Take up your **mat** and go home."

He said, "Pick up the **little rug** you were laying on. You are healed!"

Matthew 9:5–8

MATTHEW **Matthew** was a **tax collector** who became one of Jesus' twelve disciples. Matthew wrote the first book of the New Testament. He was also called "Levi."

Matthew 9:9; Luke 5:27–28

MATTHIAS **Matthias** was **one of Jesus' apostles.** He took the place of Judas Iscariot, the apostle who betrayed Jesus.

Acts 1:26

See also: Judas Iscariot

MEDES AND PERSIANS, LAW OF THE   The satraps had Daniel thrown into the lion's den by tricking king Darius. They asked him to make a rule that followed the **Law of the Medes and Persians**.

The king made a **rule that could never be changed**.

Daniel 6:15

See also: Daniel, Lion's Den, Satrap

Law of the Medes and Persians
I Darius ...

MEEK   Mary is **meek**, merciful, and pure in heart. She is **quiet, gentle, humble, patient, and kind**.

Psalm 37:11; Matthew 5:5

MELCHIZEDEK   **Melchizedek** was a **mysterious king** who knew Abraham. The Bible says Melchizedek lived forever, like Jesus.

Genesis 14:18–20; Hebrews 7:1–3

Merciful – Messenger

MERCIFUL   Mary is meek, **merciful**, and pure in heart. She is **quick to forgive** the people who hurt her.

Matthew 5:7

MESHACH   **Meshach** is a **new name for Mishael** given by king Nebuchadnezzar's servant.

King Nebuchadnezzar threw Shadrach, Meshach, and Abednego into a fiery furnace because they would not bow down and worship an idol.

Daniel 1:7, 3:1–30

MESSENGER   A **messenger** is **someone who delivers a message**. Angels are God's messengers.

Genesis 19:15;

Numbers 22:32;

Judges 6:12;

Matthew 1:20;

Luke 2:10;

Revelation 22

A messenger with a message ➤

MESSIAH   **Messiah** is a special name meaning "chosen one." Jesus is called Messiah. Jesus is **the one God chose to save people from their sins**.

John 1:40–41

METHUSELAH   **Methuselah** was Noah's grandfather. He was the **oldest man who ever lived**.

The Bible says Methuselah lived to be almost one-thousand years old!

Genesis 5:27

MICHAEL   **Michael** is an **archangel**. He is a mighty messenger sent by God.

Jude 9; Revelation 12:7

Midian – Mighty Men

MIDIAN Moses ran away from Pharaoh and went to live in **Midian**. He went to live in a **land in the Arabian Desert near the Red Sea**.

God spoke to Moses from the burning bush in the Land of Midian.

Exodus 2:15, 3:1–22

MIDWIFE A **midwife** is a woman who **helps another woman have a baby**. In the Bible, some midwives were very brave. They disobeyed the king of Egypt when he told them to kill the Israelites' babies.

Exodus 1:15–17

MIGHTY MEN Josheb, Eleazar, and Shammah were known as David's **mighty men**.

They were three **fearless soldiers** who fought at King David's side.

2 Samuel 23:8–12

A B C D E F G H I J K L **M** N O P Q R S T U V W X Y Z

MILK AND HONEY The Lord brought the children of Israel into the Promised Land—a land that flowed with **milk and honey**. He brought them into a beautiful land that had **everything they would ever need**.

Numbers 14:7–9

See also: Promised Land

MILLSTONE A **millstone** is a huge, heavy, round **stone used to grind grain** for making bread.

Luke 17:2

A millstone on a mill ➤

MINISTRY **Ministry** is **work done for God.**
Jesus set an example in ministry when He washed His disciples' feet. God wants every Christian to do some kind of ministry.

1 Timothy 1:12

Miracle – Missionary

MIRACLE   Jesus does amazing **miracles** for those who believe. When we trust Him, Jesus will gladly break every law of science and nature and do **something incredible that only God can do.**

Job 9:10; John 2:1–11, 11:1–44; Acts 9:17–18

MIRIAM   **Miriam** was **Moses' sister**. When she was young, she and her family were Hebrew slaves.

Exodus 2:1–10

MIRIAM AND JOCHEBED

The king of Egypt hated the Hebrew slaves. He said every Hebrew baby boy must die. When Moses was born, his mother Jochebed hid him in a little papyrus basket. She placed the basket along the Nile River. Miriam hid among the reeds and waited for someone to find the baby. The king's daughter found the little basket and drew Moses out of water. Miriam asked the king's daughter if she should get a Hebrew woman to feed the baby and take care of him. The king's daughter said, "Yes."

So Miriam did get someone. She got Moses' mother, Jochebed!

MISSIONARY   A **missionary** is a **person sent by God to share His love and speak His word.** You are a missionary.

Acts 12:25

Mm

MITE   A poor woman put two **mites** into the church offering.

The woman put in two **very small coins**.

Luke 21:1–4

MOAB   Ruth was born in the land of **Moab**. She was born in the land **east of the Dead Sea**.

Ruth 1:1–7

◄ *Ruth in Moab*

MOCK   The soldiers **mocked** Jesus and spat in his face. They **laughed and made fun of** him in a cruel and hateful way.

Isaiah 50:6; Matthew 27:27–31; Mark 10:33–34

Mm

Money Changers – Morning Star

MONEY CHANGERS   Jesus overturned the tables of the **money changers**. He turned over the tables of the **men who got rich by cheating people** who gave an offering in the Temple.

Matthew 21:12

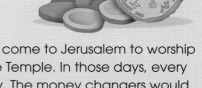

FUNNY MONEY

People from many lands would come to Jerusalem to worship God and give an offering in the Temple. In those days, every land had its own special money. The money changers would trade money from many different lands for the one kind of money that could be used for an offering in the Temple.

But they would not give the people back all of their money. The money changers would keep some of the money all for themselves.

MORDECAI   **Mordecai** was the **cousin of Queen Esther**. Mordecai raised Esther like a daughter. After she became queen, he helped protect the Jews from the evil Haman.

Esther 2:5–7, 8:1–17

MORNING STAR   The **morning star** is another name for the **day star**. You can see the day star in the eastern sky just before the sun begins to shine. Jesus said, "I am the bright, Morning Star!"

Revelation 22:16

Mm

A B C D E F G H I J K L **M** N O P Q R S T U V W X Y Z

Moses – Mount

MOSES **Moses** was the **greatest leader of God's chosen people**.

He led the Hebrew slaves out of Egypt.
He parted the Red Sea.
He wrote the first five books of the Bible.
He heard God speak from a burning bush.
He spoke with God face to face.
He received God's Ten Commandments on Mount Sinai.
He built the Tabernacle in the wilderness.

Moses loved and trusted God. And God loved and trusted him!

Exodus 2:3–12, 19–20

MOTE A **mote** is a tiny **speck of dust** or dirt.

Matthew 7:3–5

Micah has a mote in his eye ➤

MOUNT A **mount** is a **high hill**. The Bible tells of many mounts and what happened on them.

2 Peter 1:18

152

Mount Ararat – Mount Moriah

MOUNT ARARAT

Mount Ararat is the place where Noah's ark came to rest after the flood.

Genesis 8:4

See also: Flood, Noah's Ark

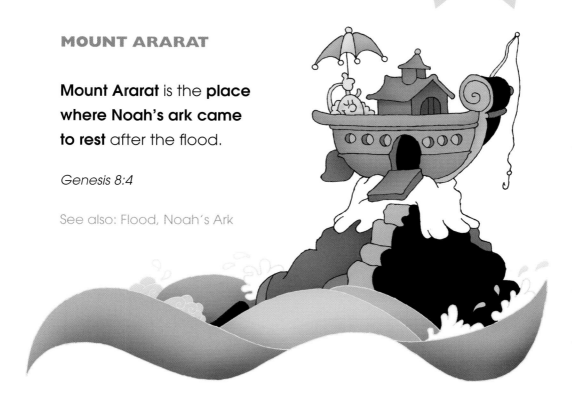

MOUNT CARMEL   Mount Carmel is the **place where Elijah defeated the prophets of Baal**.

1 Kings 18:16–39

MOUNT MORIAH   Mount Moriah is the **place where Abraham offered Isaac** and Solomon built the temple.

Genesis 22:2; 2 Chronicles 3:1

MOUNT NEBO   Mount Nebo is the **place where Moses died**. From Mount Nebo, Moses could see the Promised Land.

Deuteronomy 34:1–5

MOUNT OF OLIVES   The **Mount of Olives** is the **place where Judas Iscariot betrayed Jesus**. Jesus rose up to heaven there.

Luke 22:39–48, 24:50–51

MOUNT SINAI   Mount Sinai is the **place where God gave Moses the Ten Commandments**. God spoke to Moses from the burning bush there.

Exodus 19–20

MOURN   Rachel **mourned** the death of her children. She was **very sad and broken hearted** because her children were no more.

Matthew 2:18, 5:4

MULTITUDE   A **multitude** is a **large crowd of people**. A multitude often followed Jesus to hear His teaching and to be healed of diseases.

Matthew 4:25

Mustard Seed – Myrrh

MUSTARD SEED Jesus said, "The kingdom of God is like a **mustard seed**." In your hand, it is the **smallest seed of all**. But plant it in good ground and it will grow into the biggest plant in the entire garden.

Matthew 17:19–20; Mark 4:31

MUTE Zechariah was **mute**. He was **not able to speak**.

Luke 1:19–22

MY BROTHER'S KEEPER I will be **my brother's keeper**. I will be a **good friend who helps, trusts, and loves at all times**.

Genesis 4:9

MYRRH **Myrrh** is the dried, **sweet-smelling sap of camphor and balsam trees**. The wise men gave a gift of myrrh to the baby Jesus.

Matthew 2:11

155

NAOMI   **Naomi** was the mother of Ruth's husband.

Ruth 1–4

See also: Boaz, Ruth

RUTH AND NAOMI

Naomi was very sad. Her husband and sons died in Moab, far away from home. Ruth was very sad, too. But she loved Naomi and promised to take care of her. So they went back to Naomi's home in Bethlehem. Ruth met a man there named Boaz. He became Ruth's new husband. Boaz took good care of Ruth and Naomi for the rest of their lives.

NARD   **Nard** is a **sweet-smelling oil**, like perfume. It is made from spikenard, a leafy green plant with pink and purple flowers. Mary washed Jesus feet with a pint of pure nard.

Mark 14:3; John 12:3

NAZARETH   Jesus lived in **Nazareth** when he was a boy. He grew up in a little **village south of Cana in the land of Galilee**. In Nazareth, the angel told Mary her baby would be God's son.

Matthew 2:21–23; Luke 1:26–38

Nazarite – Nehemiah

NAZARITE Samson was a **Nazarite**. He was **a person set apart for God's special use**. Nazarites were not supposed to drink wine or cut their hair.

Judges 13:4–7

NEBUCHADNEZZAR **Nebuchadnezzar** was the **king of Babylon**. He made a huge idol and told the people to bow down and worship it. The king's servants, Shadrach, Meshach, and Abednego, would only worship the One True God. So Nebuchadnezzar threw them into a furnace filled with fire.

Nebuchadnezzar had many terrible dreams that worried him very much. God helped Daniel tell the king the meaning of his dreams.

Daniel 2–3

NEHEMIAH **Nehemiah** was a **leader of the Jewish people** who helped rebuild the city of Jerusalem. He helped God's people fix its walls, homes, and buildings. Nehemiah loved God and showed others how to get closer to Him.

Nehemiah 1–13

NEW BIRTH   Sophie asked Jesus to come into her heart. She asked Him to forgive her sins and make everything new. Jesus gave Sophie a **new birth**. She has been **born again**. Jesus erased her old life and all of its mistakes and failures. He gave her new life—a heart that loves God and wants to be more like Him.

John 3:3; 1 Peter 1:23

NEW COVENANT   The **New Covenant** is the **promise of salvation through Jesus**. God made covenants with His special people. God made special promises to the Jewish people. But His New Covenant was for all people. God said anyone can be saved by believing in Jesus!

Jeremiah 31:31–34; Luke 22:20

NEW TESTAMENT   The **New Testament** is the **second part of the Bible**. It tells about Jesus and all the good things He said and did. It also tells us He is coming back one day very soon!

BOOKS OF THE NEW TESTAMENT

Matthew	Ephesians	Hebrews
Mark	Philippians	James
Luke	Colossians	1 Peter
John	1 Thessalonians	2 Peter
Acts	2 Thessalonians	1 John
Romans	1 Timothy	2 John
1 Corinthians	2 Timothy	3 John
2 Corinthians	Titus	Jude
Galatians	Philemon	Revelation

New Wine – Nile River

NEW WINE   Jesus said, "**New wine** must be poured into new wineskins." He said, "The **beautiful, new life only God can give** must be poured into a clean, new heart that is ready and willing to be filled with good things.

Luke 5:37–38

See also: Wineskin

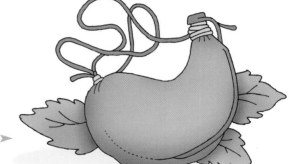

A wineskin filled with new wine ➤

NICODEMUS   **Nicodemus** was a **Pharisee who wanted to know more about Jesus**. "You must be born again," Jesus told him. "But how?" Nicodemus asked. "Can a man go back into his mother's belly?" "Of course not," Jesus replied. "You must allow Me to be born in your heart."

John 3:1–21

NILE RIVER   The **Nile River** is the **biggest river in Egypt**. Jochebed put baby Moses in a basket in the Nile River to protect him from the king.

Exodus 2:1–10

Nn

NINEVEH   When the fish spat out Jonah, he began to preach to the people of **Nineveh**. He told the people who lived in the **large, wealthy capital city of Assyria** that they were very, very naughty and God wanted them to change.

Jonah 3:2

Jonah in Nineveh ➤

NOAH   **Noah** and his sons **built the ark**. They built a huge boat to rescue their family and all of God's creatures.

God told Noah a great flood was coming that would cover the whole earth.

STEP 1.

Noah did not know how to build a boat. He didn't even live near the water!

But Noah trusted God and did what God said. So life on earth was saved.

Genesis 6:9–9:17

Noah's Ark – Nod

NOAH'S ARK   **Noah's ark** was the **huge boat Noah built** to save his family from the flood. Noah's sons Shem, Ham, and Japheth helped him build the ark.

Genesis 6:9–9:17

See also: Flood, Rainbow

ALL ABOUT NOAH'S ARK

Noah's ark was 450 feet long, 75 feet wide, and 45 feet high.

It took Noah and his sons a long time to build the ark. How long? No one knows for sure. But here's a clue: God's Word says Noah was 500 years old when his sons were born, and 600 years old when the flood began.

Noah took two of every living creature into the ark, just as God asked. When the flood finally came, it rained for forty days and forty nights. The ark came to rest on the top of Mount Ararat. When the floodwater went back down, only Noah, his family, and the animals on the ark were saved!

NOD   **Nod** was a place **east of the Garden of Eden**. Adam and Eve's son Cain went there after he killed his brother, Abel.

Genesis 4:16

ABCDEFGHIJKLMN**O**PQRSTUVWXYZ

O

OFFERING Sophie gave an **offering**. Sophie gave God a **special gift** to thank Him for all the good things He's done.

Ephesians 5:1–2

OFFSPRING Cain and Abel are the **offspring** of Adam and Eve. Cain and Abel are Adam and Eve's **children**.

Genesis 22:18

OIL Leah filled her lamp with **oil** so its light would not go out.

She filled her lamp with the clear, thick **liquid from pressed olives**.

Leviticus 24:2

A lamp filled with olive oil ➤

OLD TESTAMENT   The **Old Testament** is the **first part of the Bible**. The Old Testament is made up of thirty-nine books, starting with Genesis and ending with Malachi. The Old Testament is the story of God's work before Jesus was born.

2 Corinthians 3:14

OLIVE   An **olive** is a small **round fruit with a hard pit**.

Olives are green before they are ripe. They turn dark brown or black when they are ready to eat. Olives are used for food. They are also used to make oil.

Deuteronomy 28:40; Psalm 52:8

OLIVE BRANCH   An **olive branch** is the **woody limb of an olive tree**. When the dove gave Noah a leaf from an olive branch, Noah knew the water had gone back down. The flood was finally over!

Genesis 8:11

Oo

ORPAH   **Orpah** was **Naomi's daughter-in-law**.

Orpah and Ruth were each married to a son of Naomi. Naomi was very sad when her sons died. She asked Orpah and Ruth to go back to their parents' homes. Orpah left Naomi. But Ruth would not. Ruth stayed with Naomi and took care of her for the rest of her life.

Ruth 1:14

See also: Boaz, Naomi, Ruth

OVERCOME   To **overcome** is to **win**! When we have faith in God, we will overcome the trouble and sin in the world.

1 John 5:4

OX   Obed is as strong as an **ox**. He is as strong as a **full-grown bull** or cow. A farmer uses more than one ox to pull heavy carts or plows.

Deuteronomy 25:4

A pair of oxen ➤

Pp

Palace – Papyrus

PALACE   Solomon lived in the royal **palace.** Solomon lived in a large, beautiful **house made just for the king.**

1 Kings 9:1–3

See also: Solomon

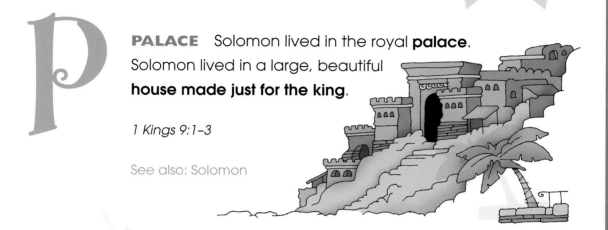

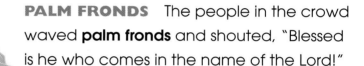

PALM FRONDS   The people in the crowd waved **palm fronds** and shouted, "Blessed is he who comes in the name of the Lord!"

Palm fronds are the **leafy branches of a palm tree.**

John 12:13

PAPYRUS   **Papyrus** is another name for **bulrushes.** Moses' mother made a basket from papyrus.

She made a basket from tall plants, like cattails, that grow near the water.

Exodus 2:3

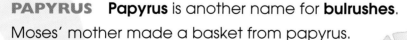

A B C D E F G H I J K L M N O P Q R S T U V W X Y Z

PARABLE Jesus taught the children with a **parable**. He told them a **short, simple story** with familiar words and pictures to help them learn an important lesson.

Matthew 13:3

THE PARABLES OF JESUS

Here are a few of Jesus' parables and where you can find them.

The Lost Sheep	Luke 15:4–7
The Lost Coin	Luke 15:8–10
The Prodigal Son	Luke 15:11–32
The Good Samaritan	Luke 10:25–37
The Good Shepherd	John 10:1–18
The Vineyard Workers	Matthew 20:1–16
The Pharisee and the Tax Collector	Luke 18:9–14
The Seed and the Sower	Matthew 13:3–9
The Wise Builder	Matthew 7:24–27
The Ten Talents	Matthew 25:14–30
The Ten Lamps	Matthew 25:1–13

PARADISE Jesus told the thief on the cross, "Today you will be with me in **paradise**." He said, "I tell you the truth, today we will be together in **heaven**."

Luke 23:43

PARALYTIC Jesus healed the **paralytic**. He healed the man who was paralyzed, and **could not move his arms or legs**.

Matthew 9:1–8

PARDON The sinful man asked God for a **pardon**. He asked God for **forgiveness**. God loves to forgive people who turn away from sin.

Isaiah 55:7

PASSOVER Jesus and the disciples celebrated the **Passover**. They celebrated a **special holiday** to help them remember how God set His children free from slavery and led them out of Egypt into the Promised Land.

Exodus 12:13; Matthew 26:19

See also: Exodus, Promised Land

PATMOS **Patmos** is a little **island in the Aegean Sea** that the Romans used as a prison. John wrote the book of Revelation while he was imprisoned on Patmos.

Revelation 1:9

167

Pp

PAUL **Paul** was an **apostle**. He spread the good news about Jesus all over the world.

Many of the books in the New Testament were written by the apostle Paul.

Acts 13:1; 1 Timothy 1:1–2

A CHANGE OF HEART

Before Paul met Jesus, his name was Saul.

Saul was a Pharisee. He was a very religious man. But Saul hated Jesus. He threatened to kill Jesus' followers and sent many of them to prison.

Did God punish Saul for this? No! He did something much better. Jesus met Saul on the road to Damascus and changed his heart!

Acts 9:1-19

PEACE **Peace** is the **quiet, happy feeling only God can give.** People who argue and fight are not full of peace. Jesus said He would give all His children peace.

John 14:27

Pearl of Great Price – Persecute

PEARL OF GREAT PRICE   The merchant sold everything to buy the **Pearl of Great Price**.

When he found **the very best thing of all**, he sold everything he had to make it his own.

Jesus is the Pearl of Great Price.

Matthew 13:45–46

PENTECOST   The disciples were filled with the Holy Spirit on the day of **Pentecost**. They were filled with God's power **fifty days after Passover**, when Jesus died on the cross.

Acts 2:1–4

PERSECUTE   Unbelievers like to **persecute** Priscilla because of her faith. They **say and do cruel and hurtful things because she loves Jesus**.

Jesus told us to pray for the people who persecute us.

Matthew 5:10–12, 44

Pp

PERSEVERANCE **Perseverance** is being **able to keep going when times are tough.** Jesus wants His children to have perseverance.

James 1:2–4

PETER **Peter** was a fisherman. He was **leader of the twelve disciples,** and one of Jesus' very best friends.

Peter loved Jesus with all his heart. He did many amazing things. Peter healed a man who could not walk. He raised a woman from the dead. He even walked on the water. Peter made a lot of mistakes, too. But Jesus never gave up on him.

He called Peter The Rock. "And on this rock," Jesus said, "I will build My church."

Matthew 14:28–31, 16:18, 26:75; Acts 3:6, 9:40–42

PETITION Esther made a **petition** to the king to spare her people. She made a **special request** to the king asking him to let her people live.

Esther 7:1–3

PHARAOH   In Bible times, **Pharaoh** was a special **name for the king of Egypt**.

The king of Egypt forced God's people to live as slaves. Moses told Pharaoh to let God's people go. But the king would not. So God sent ten terrible plagues on the people of Egypt.

Exodus 7:1–12:31

PHARISEE   The **Pharisees** were the **religious leaders and teachers** in Jesus' day.

The Pharisees loved rules. They became very angry when people broke them. Jesus said the Pharisees were like a cup that was kept spotlessly clean on the outside, but never, ever washed on the inside.

Matthew 12:2–14, 23:24

See also: Sadducee

PHILISTINES   The **Philistines** were the **enemies of Israel**. They hated God's people and wanted to harm them.

2 Samuel 5:17–25

PHYLACTERY A **phylactery** is a **little box with Bible verses inside**. A religious man tied this box around his head or arm. It reminded him to do what God said.

Matthew 23:5

See also: Pharisee

PHYSICIAN A person who takes care of sick people is called a **physician**. A physician is a **doctor**. He tries to help sick people feel better.

Matthew 9:12

PILATE Pontius **Pilate** was the **Roman governor of Judea**. He was the man in charge of the place called Judea.

Pilate handed Jesus over to die on the cross.

Matthew 27:11–26

PILLAR OF FIRE AND CLOUDS   A **pillar** is a **tall pole or post** that stands straight up and down. God made a pillar of fire appear in the night sky so His children could follow Him to the Promised Land. In the day He made a pillar of clouds so they would know the right way to go.

Exodus 13:21

PILLAR OF SALT   "Run away! Don't stop and don't look back!" the angel said. "God is about to destroy the cities of Sodom and Gomorrah!" So Lot and his family ran away.

But Lot's wife stopped and looked back! Burning sulfur rained down from heaven. **Lot's wife** turned into a **Pillar of Salt**.

Genesis 19:26

See also: Lot, Sodom and Gomorrah

PITCH   **Pitch** is a kind of **sticky, black tar**. Noah covered the ark with pitch. He put tar on the outside of the ark so it would not leak.

Genesis 6:14

A pot filled with pitch ➤

PITY The Good Samaritan saw a man lying beside the road and took **pity** on him. He **felt very sorry** because the man was in pain. The Good Samaritan decided to stop and help.

Luke 10:33

PLAGUE A **plague** is a time of **very bad sickness or trouble**. God sent ten plagues on the people of Egypt.

THE TEN PLAGUES OF EGYPT

The story of the Ten Plagues is found in Exodus chapters 7 through 11.

1. Water turned to blood
2. Frogs
3. Lice
4. Flies
5. Farm animals got sick
6. Boils and sores
7. Hail
8. Locusts
9. Darkness for three days
10. Death of firstborn

God sent ten plagues on Egypt because Pharaoh would not let God's children go free.

Exodus 7–11

See also: Chosen People, Pharaoh

Frogs ➤

Plowshare – Poor

PLOWSHARE A **plowshare** is the **strong iron blade on a plow**.

A farmer uses a plow to turn over the soil to prepare it for planting.

1 Samuel 13:20

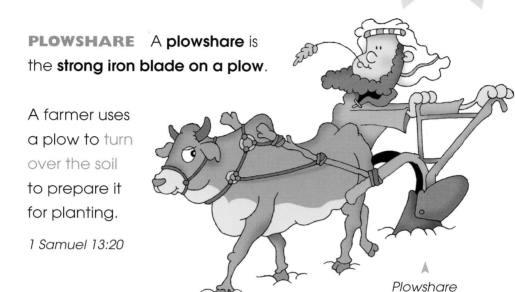

Plowshare

PLUMB LINE A **plumb line** is a **builder's tool** with a small weight attached to a string.

A carpenter uses a plumb line to make sure his work stands up straight. He uses it to make sure his work is not crooked.

Amos 7:7–9

POOR To be **poor** means you do **not have a lot of money or things**. Jesus wants us to help people who are poor.

Luke 14:13–14

POTIPHAR   **Potiphar** was a **ruler in Egypt**. He threw his slave Joseph into prison for a crime he did not commit.

Genesis 39:1–20

See also: Joseph

POTSHERD   Job picked up a **potsherd** and sat down in a pile of ashes. He took a **piece of broken of pottery** and began to scratch his painful sores.

Job 2:8

See also: Job

Potsherds ➤

POTTAGE   **Pottage** is **thick soup** cooked in a pot. It is a stew made from vegetables and meat.

Genesis 25:29–34

Potter – Preach

POTTER   A person who **uses his hands to make pots, dishes, and bowls out of clay** is called a **potter**. The Bible says, "God is the potter. We are the clay." We are the work of God's hands.

Isaiah 64:8

Clay pot made by a potter ➤

PRAISE   God's people **praise** Him. God's people **sing and give thanks** to Him.

Psalm 42:4

PRAYER   **Prayer** is **talking to God**.

When you tell God how you feel, you are praying. When you ask Him for the things you need, you are praying.

James 5:16

PREACH   Paul liked to **preach** to the people in Rome. He liked to **stand up and tell the good news** about Jesus.

Isaiah 61:1

Pp

PREFECT A **prefect** is a **man in charge** of people, places or things.

Daniel 3:2

See also: Satrap

PRIDE Hazor's heart was filled with **pride**. He **thought he was smarter, better, and more important** than everyone else.

Proverbs 16:18

PRIEST A **priest** is a **religious leader**.

In the Old Testament, priests made sacrifices. Priests gave animals to God for the people's sin. Jesus became the last sacrifice for sin when He died on the cross. Now Jesus is our "Great High Priest."

Exodus 29; Hebrews 7:26–28

Prodigal Son – Promised Land

PRODIGAL SON   Jesus sat down for dinner with the outlaws, troublemakers, and sinners and told them the story of the **Prodigal Son**.

He told about a **son who ran away from home** and did many foolish things. He told them how much the father loved his son and wanted him to come back home.

Luke 15:11–32

PROMISE   God will never leave you or take His love away. That is a **promise**. It is **something God said, that He will surely do**.

2 Corinthians 1:20; 2 Peter 3:9; 1 John 2:25

PROMISED LAND   The children of Israel entered the **Promised Land**. Joshua led them into Canaan—the **land God promised to Abraham and his offspring**. It was a good land that flowed with milk and honey.

Genesis 12:7, 13:15, 15:18; Joshua 1:1–3

Pp

PROPHECY   A **prophecy** is a **message from God**. Some Bible prophecies tell what is going to happen in the future. Some prophecies are things God wants people to do right now.

Romans 12:6

PROPHET   Jeremiah was a **prophet**. He was a man who **spoke God's words to the people**.

Jeremiah 1:5

PROSTRATE   The false prophets fell **prostrate** before Elijah. They fell **on their faces with their arms and legs stretched out wide**.

1 Kings 18:39; Daniel 2:46

PROVERBS   King Solomon wrote down many **proverbs**. He wrote many **short, helpful sayings that speak the truth** and give good advice.

Proverbs 1–31

180

Prune – Psalmist

PRUNE The farmer **pruned** his vines.

He **cut back their leaves and branches** to make the plants stronger. Jesus said that God prunes His people. He said God will take things out of our lives to make us better and stronger.

John 15:1–2

PSALM A **psalm** is a beautiful **song of worship and praise** to God.

Psalms 1–150

PSALMIST King David was a **psalmist**.

He was a man who **wrote, sang, and played beautiful songs** of worship and praise.

2 Samuel 23:1

Qq

Q

QUAIL The **quail** is a **small bird** with a short tail and brown feathers.

When the Israelites grumbled and complained about the manna God gave them to eat, God became angry and covered the ground with quail.

Exodus 16:13

QUEEN A **queen** is a **woman who rules a country**. A queen might be the wife of a king, like Bathsheba or Esther. Or a queen might rule a country by herself.

Esther 5:2

QUEEN OF SHEBA The **Queen of Sheba** came from a far-away land to **test king Solomon with many hard questions**.

She saw the wisdom God gave to Solomon. She gave Solomon many gifts and praised the Lord for the good things he had done.

1 Kings 10:1–13

Quicken – Quiver

QUICKEN **Quicken** me according to your word, O Lord. Let your word **spring to life** deep down in my heart.

Psalm 119:154, 159

QUIVER A **quiver** is the **leather bag an archer carries** to hold his arrows.

Psalm 127:4–5

A B C D E F G H I J K L M N O P Q R S T U V W X Y Z

Rr

RABBI A **rabbi** is a **teacher**. "Rabbi" is a respectful name. When Nicodemus visited Jesus at night, he called Jesus "*Rabbi.*"

John 3:1–2

RACHEL **Rachel** was **Jacob's wife**. Jacob worked for Laban fourteen years so he could marry Rachel.

Genesis 29:11, 26–30

See also: Jacob, Laban

RAHAB **Rahab** was the **woman who hid the spies** Joshua sent to Jericho.

When the walls fell down, Joshua's men rescued Rahab and her family. Then the army rushed in and destroyed Jericho and everything in it.

Joshua 2:1–24, 6:22

Rainbow – Ram's Horn

RAINBOW   After the rain stopped, the sun came out, and Noah saw a **rainbow**.

He saw a **beautiful arch of colors in the sky**.

The colors of the rainbow are red, orange, yellow, green, blue, indigo, and violet.

Genesis 9:16

RAM   A **ram** is a **male sheep with big, curly horns**.

In Bible times, people used rams as a sacrifice to God. People would give God a gift of a ram.

Exodus 29:15–22

RAM'S HORN   The priests blew a **ram's horn** and the walls of Jericho fell down. They blew **trumpets made from the curly horns of a male sheep**.

Joshua 6:4

See also: Shofar

185

RAMESES   The Hebrew slaves built the city of **Rameses**.

They were forced to build a **city in Egypt** with sun-dried bricks made from mud and straw.

Exodus 1:11

RANSOM   Jesus gave His life as a **ransom** for many. He paid **the price to set us free** from our sins.

Mark 10:45

RAPTURE   The **rapture** will be **part of Jesus' second coming**. The rapture will happen when God takes His people up into the sky. There they will meet Jesus in the clouds!

1 Thessalonians 4:16–17

See also: Second Coming

REAP The Bible says we will **reap** what we sow. We will **cut, pick, or gather the crops** we have planted.

Leviticus 19:9; Galatians 6:7

See also: Sow

REBEKAH **Rebekah** was **Isaac's wife**. She was the mother of Jacob and Esau.

Genesis 25:20–26

RECONCILE Jacob and Esau needed to **reconcile** with each other. God helped them **come back together**.

They forgave each other and became friends once again.

Genesis 33:1–15; Matthew 5:24

RED SEA   The **Red Sea** is a **body of water east of Egypt**. God parted the Red Sea to let His people cross on dry land.

God made the water split in two so His people could walk through. Then the water rushed back together and swept Pharaoh's army away like a flood.

Exodus 14:21–22, 15:3–5

REDEEMER   Jesus is our **redeemer**. He pays the price and **buys us back** from the punishment we deserve for our sin.

Job 19:25; Isaiah 59:20; 1 Peter 1:18

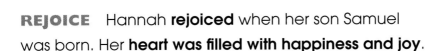

REJOICE   Hannah **rejoiced** when her son Samuel was born. Her **heart was filled with happiness and joy**.

1 Samuel 2:1

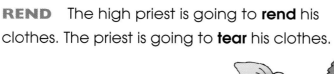

Remnant – Repent

REMNANT   There is still a **remnant** that loves God with all of their heart. There are still **a few people left** who love God with all of their heart.

Isaiah 28:5; Romans 11:5

REND   The high priest is going to **rend** his clothes. The priest is going to **tear** his clothes.

In the Bible, people would rend their clothes when they were very sad or *very* angry.

2 Samuel 3:31

REPENT   Jonah told the people of Nineveh to **repent**. He told them to change their minds and **turn away from sin**.

When the people saw that they were wrong, they all felt sorry and began to change.

Jonah 3:10; Luke 15:10

Jonah told the people to repent ➤

Rr

RESURRECT Jesus said He would **resurrect** from the dead. He **would come back to life** three days after He died on the cross.

John 11:25

REUBEN **Reuben** was the oldest son of Jacob and Leah. He was **Jacob's firstborn son**.

Genesis 35:23

REVELATION God gave John a **revelation**.

God **uncovered His truth** to John so he could write it down for others in the Bible. The last book of the Bible is called "Revelation."

Revelation 1:1

REVERENCE **Reverence** is a deep **feeling of respect and devotion** for someone or something.

2 Corinthians 7:1

Rhoda – Risen

RHODA **Rhoda** was a servant girl. She was the **helper of Mary the mother of John**.

When an angel let Peter out of prison, he went to Mary's house. Peter pounded on the door and asked to come inside. Rhoda recognized Peter's voice, but she was so excited she forgot to let Peter in!

Acts 12:12–14

RICH YOUNG RULER The **rich young ruler** kept all of God's Ten Commandments. He **asked Jesus what to do to have eternal life**. Jesus told him to sell everything he had! He told the young ruler to give the money to the poor and then come follow Him.

Luke 18:18–25

RIGHTEOUS Paul believes in Jesus. He is **righteous**. He is **right with God**.

1 John 3:7

RISEN Jesus has **risen**, just as He said! He **was dead and buried, but now He is alive** and well!

Matthew 28:6

RIVER OF LIFE The angel showed John the **River of Life** flowing from the throne of God.

John saw a **vision of God's love and power** like a beautiful dream. Where the River of Life flows, everything comes alive!

Ezekiel 47:1–12; Revelation 22:1

ROBE A **robe** is a long, loose fitting piece of **clothing**.

Mark 15:17

ROME **Rome** is a **city in Italy**. During Jesus' time, Rome was the most powerful city on earth. Soldiers from Rome put Jesus on the cross. Many of Jesus' disciples were arrested by soldiers from Rome. The apostle Paul went to Rome to tell people about Jesus.

Romans 1:7

Rooster – Ruth

ROOSTER   A **rooster** is an **adult male chicken**. A female chicken is called a hen.

John 13:38

ROOT   A **root** is **part of a plant** that holds it firmly in the ground.

Proverbs 12:12

RUDDY   David was **ruddy** and handsome. His skin had a natural, **healthy red glow**.

1 Samuel 17:42

RUTH   **Ruth** was a loyal **daughter-in-law to Naomi**. Their story became a book in the Bible.

Ruth stayed with Naomi after both of their husbands died. When Ruth married again, she had a son who had a son who had a son named King David.

Ruth 1–4

A B C D E F G H I J K L M N O P Q **R** S T U V W X Y Z

Ss

SABBATH   The **Sabbath** is a **holy day of rest** for God's children. The Israelites celebrated the Sabbath on Saturday.

Exodus 20:8–11

SABBATH DAY'S JOURNEY   A **Sabbath day's journey** is **the distance a Jewish person was allowed to travel on the Sabbath**. It is the distance from Jerusalem to the Mount of Olives—a little less than one mile.

Acts 1:12

SACKCLOTH   **Sackcloth** is a **rough fabric** made from coarse, prickly goat's hair, hemp, or flax.

People wore sackcloth when they were very sad, or when they wanted to show God they were sorry for their sins.

Job 16:15; Lamentations 2:10

194

Sacrifice – Saints

SACRIFICE   A **sacrifice** is an **offering to God**.

God's people used to sacrifice animals after they sinned. But Jesus was the last sacrifice. His offering to God was enough to pay for the sins of the whole world!

Exodus 5:3; Hebrews 7:22–27

SADDUCEES   The **Sadducees** were the **religious leaders and teachers in Jesus' day**.

The Sadducees did not believe in life after death. But Jesus did. And He came back to life to prove it.

Mark 12:18

See also: Pharisee

SAINTS   The **saints** are a large group of **people everywhere** around the world who love Jesus and are born again.

Psalm 30:4, 149:1; Romans 8:27; Philemon 7; Revelation 8:4

Ss

Salt and Light – Samaritan

SALT AND LIGHT Jesus said **you** are the **salt and light** this dark and hungry world needs.

You are the salt of the earth. Your life makes everything it touches taste better.

You are the light of the world. Don't hide your light. Shine it so everyone can see!

Matthew 5:13–16

SALVATION Everyone needs **salvation**. Everyone needs God to **take away their sin**. Jesus is the only way to salvation. When we believe in Jesus, God makes us part of His family. Salvation is a gift from God!

Acts 4:12

SAMARITAN A **Samaritan** is a **person from Samaria**.

The Jews hated the Samaritans. But Jesus did not. He told them about the Good Samaritan, a man from Samaria who stopped to help a Jew when his own Jewish brothers would not!

Luke 10:25–37

Samson – Sanctuary

SAMSON   **Samson** was a **mighty man of God**. His long hair gave him power and strength.

Samson loved Delilah. But Delilah did not love Samson. Delilah cut off Samson's hair so his power and strength would be gone!

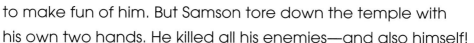

Samson's enemies captured him and threw him in prison. They brought Samson to the temple to make fun of him. But Samson tore down the temple with his own two hands. He killed all his enemies—and also himself!

Judges 16:4–31

SAMUEL   **Samuel** was a **leader of Israel**. God called him to lead when he was just a boy. Samuel helped God's people turn away from idols and enjoy great peace.

1 Samuel 2:26, 3:19–20, 7:15–17

SANCTUARY   A **sanctuary** is a **safe place**. A sanctuary is also a place where people meet for church.

Psalm 73:17; Ezekiel 11:16

SANDALS Sandals are light, **open-toed shoes** held to the foot with straps.

Exodus 3:5

SANHEDRIN The chief priests called a meeting of the **Sanhedrin**. They called for a meeting of the **high court and its leaders, the Pharisees, the Sadducees, and the high priest**.

John 11:47

SAPPHIRE Ezekiel saw a throne made of **sapphire**, and above it, the figure of a man! He saw a throne made of beautiful, clear, **dark blue stones**.

Ezekiel 1:26

See also: Throne

Sarah – Saul

SARAH Sarah was the **wife of Abraham**.

For many years, Sarah could not have a baby. But God promised Abraham that Sarah would have a son. When she was ninety years old, Sarah gave birth to Isaac!

Hebrews 11:8–11

SATAN Satan is another name for the **devil**.

Isaiah 14:12–17; Luke 10:18; Romans 16:20; James 4:7; 1 Peter 5:8

SATRAP A **satrap** was a low ranking, dishonest **ruler controlled by the king**.

Daniel 3:2

SAUL Before the **apostle Paul** met Jesus on the Damascus Road, his name was **Saul**.

Acts 9:1–19

SAUL, KING   **King Saul** was the **first king of Israel**.

Saul became selfish. So God decided to make David king of Israel instead of Saul.

1 Samuel 9–10, 13:1–14

SAVE   Jesus is the only one who can **save** us from our sins. He is the only one who can **rescue us and keep us safe from harm**.

John 3:17; Acts 4:12; Romans 10:13

SAVIOR   Jesus is our **savior**. He is the one who **saves us from our sins** by His death on the cross.

Luke 2:11

SCEPTER   A **scepter** is a **king's staff or rod**. Like a crown, it shows the people who is king.

Esther 5:2

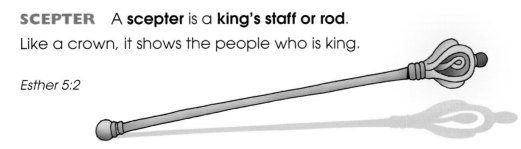

Scourge – Scroll

SCOURGE   A **scourge** is a kind of **whip**. Soldiers hit Jesus with a scourge before they nailed Him to the cross.

Matthew 27:26

SCRIBE   A **scribe** was a **person who copied books and letters by hand** so others could read them.

Nehemiah 8:1

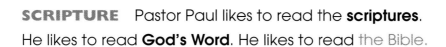

SCRIPTURE   Pastor Paul likes to read the **scriptures**. He likes to read **God's Word**. He likes to read the Bible.

Luke 24:32

SCROLL   Jesus read from the **scroll** of the prophet Isaiah.

He read from a **roll of paper** used for writing or painting.

Luke 4:17; Revelation 5:9

Ss

SEA OF GALILEE The **Sea of Galilee** is a large **lake in Israel**. Jesus lived on the edge of the Sea of Galilee, in a town called Capernaum. Once, Jesus stopped a storm on the Sea of Galilee. All He had to do was speak the words, "Peace! Be still!"

Mark 4:35–41

SEAL A **seal** is a **special mark** that shows who owns something. When we believe in Jesus, God marks us with a seal—His Holy Spirit!

Ephesians 1:13

SECOND COMING One day **Jesus will come back to earth**. He will take His children home. No one knows when. Only God knows for sure. But Jesus will come! That day is called the **second coming**.

Matthew 24:36, 42, 44; John 14:1–3

SEPULCHER Joseph and Nicodemus wrapped Jesus' body in strips of linen and laid Him in a **sepulcher**.

They placed Jesus' body in a **grave**.

John 19:41

Seraphim – Servant

SERAPHIM **Seraphim** are **angels with six wings**. Seraphim fly above God's throne and sing praise to the Lord.

Isaiah 6:1–3

SERMON ON THE MOUNT Jesus preached the **Sermon on the Mount.**

On a hillside near the Sea of Galilee, many people gathered to hear Jesus. He **taught many things about God's kindness and love**.

Matthew 5–7

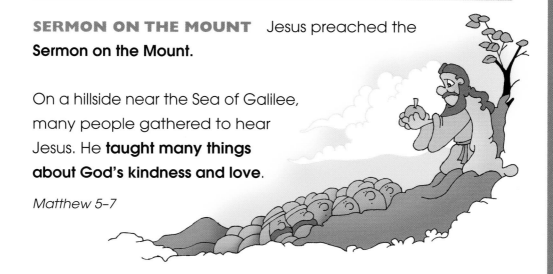

SERPENT A **serpent** is a **snake**. It is a long reptile with no arms or legs that crawls on its belly. The serpent is also another name for Satan.

Genesis 3:4; Revelation 12:9

SERVANT A **servant** is s**omeone who serves others**. It is someone who helps others when help is needed most.

Philippians 2:7

A B C D E F G H I J K L M N O P Q R S T U V W X Y Z

Ss

SEVEN CHURCHES   The **seven churches** were seven **groups of Christians** in Asia Minor. In the book of Revelation, Jesus had a message for each church. Some were doing well. Others needed to love and trust Jesus more.

Revelation 2–3

SEVEN SEALS, BOOK OF THE   John wrote the **Book of Revelation**. He wrote the **Book of the Seven Seals**. The Seven Seals are seven warnings about things to come.

Revelation 1–22

SHACKLES   Samson was bound with bronze **shackles**. He wore **chains on his ankles and wrists** so he could not fight or run away.

Judges 16:21

SHADRACH   **Shadrach** was a man who lived through a terrible fire. Shadrach and two friends—Meshach and Abednego—**would not worship a golden statue**. So the king threw them into a blazing furnace. But God protected all three!

Daniel 3

Sheaves – Sheep's Clothing

SHEAVES   Sheaves are **stalks of grain** bundled and tied together after they have been cut.

Ruth 2:7

See also: Reap

SHEEP   A **sheep** is a small **farm animal** with a thick, woolly coat. Farmers raise sheep for wool and meat. A group of sheep is called a flock.

Isaiah 53:6–7; Matthew 18:12–13

SHEEP'S CLOTHING   Jesus said a false prophet is a like a wolf in **sheep's clothing**.

He is like a dangerous, wild animal **pretending to be loving, gentle, and kind**.

Matthew 7:15

205

Ss

SHEKEL   A **shekel** is a **measure of weight** used in Bible times. People used the shekel of silver as a kind of money.

Genesis 23:12–16

SHELTER   A **shelter** is a **place that covers and protects**. A shelter **keeps you safe** from harm.

Psalm 31:20

A shelter made of sticks ➤

SHEM   **Shem** was **one of Noah's sons**. Shem helped Noah build the ark.

Genesis 7:13

See also: , Ham, Japheth, Noah, Noah's Ark

SHEPHERD   A **shepherd** is a person who **takes care of sheep**. When he was a boy, King David was a shepherd.

1 Samuel 17:15; Psalm 23:1; John 10:11

SHEWBREAD   **Shewbread** is a name for the **unleavened bread** placed on a table in the tabernacle every Sabbath day.

Exodus 25:30

See also: Tabernacle

SHOFAR   The priests sounded the **shofar,**

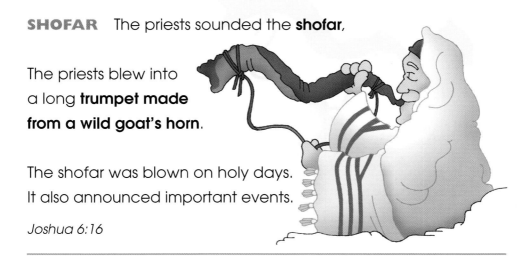

The priests blew into a long **trumpet made from a wild goat's horn.**

The shofar was blown on holy days. It also announced important events.

Joshua 6:16

SIGN   The rainbow is a **sign** of God's covenant.

It is a **reminder of God's promise** never to cover the earth with a flood again. A sign can also be a miracle that proves God means what He says.

Genesis 9:13; Numbers 14:22–24

SIGNET RING The king wore a **signet ring**. He wore a **ring with a special design**.

Sometimes kings would press their signet rings into wax or clay on a message. The design proved the message came from the king.

Jeremiah 22:24

SILAS Paul and **Silas** were missionaries. They **went many places to tell people about Jesus**. They even went to prison!

Did Paul and Silas get upset? No! They sang hymns and praised God. The earth shook. The prison doors flew open. Then the man who put Paul and Silas in prison asked them what he needed to do to get saved—and he did!

Acts 16:22–34

SILOAM Jesus healed a blind man at the pool of **Siloam**. The pool of Siloam was fed by an underground spring. It **provided cool water** for the people of Jerusalem.

John 9:7

Simon of Cyrene – Sinews

SIMON OF CYRENE Simon of Cyrene was forced to **carry Jesus' cross** up the long hill to Golgotha.

Mark 15:21

See also: Golgotha

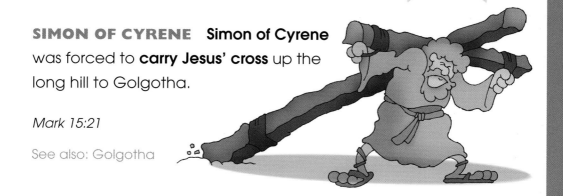

SIN Sin is **disobedience to God**. Adam and Eve were the first people to sin. They ate fruit God had told them not to eat. Since that time, every person has sinned. God hates and punishes sin. But Jesus died on the cross to take the punishment for sin. Anyone who believes in Jesus can be saved from sin!

Romans 5:12–15

SIN OFFERING A **sin offering** was a **sacrifice to pay for the sins of the people**. A priest took fat and inner parts of a healthy young bull and burned them on the altar in a smoky fire.

Exodus 30:10; Leviticus 4:13–21

SINEWS Sinews are the tough, white tissues that **connect muscles to bones**. Sinews and muscles work together to give us our strength.

Job 40:17

SLAVE   A **slave** is a **person who is forced to work** for another person for no pay. The Israelites were the slaves of Pharaoh.

Exodus 6:6

SLING   A **sling** is a **weapon that throws stones**. David used a sling to kill the giant Goliath.

1 Samuel 17:50

SLUGGARD   Seymore is a **sluggard**. He is **a very lazy person** who does not like to work.

Proverbs 6:6, 13:4

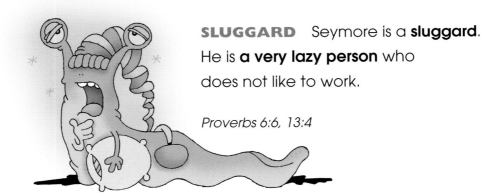

SODOM AND GOMORRAH   Lot and his family fled from **Sodom and Gomorrah**. They ran away from the **two evil cities God destroyed** with fire and brimstone.

Genesis 19:24

See also: Brimstone

Sojourn – Son of Man

SOJOURN   Elimelech and Naomi **sojourned** in Moab. They went to the city of Moab and **stayed for a short time**.

Ruth 1:1

SOLOMON   **Solomon** was the **wisest person who ever lived**.

Solomon was the son of King David and became king of Israel when David died. He asked God for wisdom, and God made Solomon smarter than anyone else. But Solomon still made mistakes—like marrying seven hundred wives!

1 Kings 4:30–31

SON OF GOD   **Jesus** is the **Son of God**. His mother was Mary. Mary's husband was Joseph. But Jesus' Father is God.

Mark 1:1; Luke 1:35

SON OF MAN   **Jesus** is the **Son of Man**.

Jesus stepped out of heaven and became a man like us. He died on the cross so we could step into heaven and be with Him.

Luke 9:22

SONS OF THUNDER   Jesus called His disciples **James and John** the **sons of thunder**. Jesus gave James and John a nickname that told something about them.

Mark 3:17

SORCERY   **Sorcery** is a **kind of magic**. Sorcery tries to use the devil's power to hurt others or fill their hearts with fear. God wants His children to stay far away from magic and sorcery.

Deuteronomy 18:10

SOUL   God gave each of us a spirit, a body, and a **soul**. Our spirit is who we are. Our body is where we live. Our soul is **what we think and feel**.

1 Thessalonians 5:23

SOW   The farmer went out to **sow** his seed. He went out to **plant** his seed in the ground.

Matthew 13:3

Sower – Spikenard

SOWER   A **sower** is a man who sows seed. He is a farmer who **plants seeds in the ground and helps them grow**.

Isaiah 55:10–11

SPARROW   A **sparrow** is a **little, brown bird** found just about everywhere. Jesus said God knows every sparrow on earth. And Jesus said you are much more valuable than sparrows!

Matthew 10:28–31

SPEAR   A **spear** is a **weapon** with a long shaft and a sharp, pointed tip. Goliath came against David with a sword and a spear.

1 Samuel 17:45

SPIKENARD   **Spikenard** is an expensive, sweet-smelling **spice used to make perfume**. A woman named Mary washed Jesus' feet with spikenard.

John 12:3

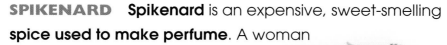

213

A B C D E F G H I J K L M N O P Q R **S** T U V W X Y Z

Ss

SPIRIT   God gave each of us a **spirit**, a soul, and a body. Our spirit is who we are on the inside. It is **the part of us that will live forever**.

1 Thessalonians 5:23

SPIRIT OF GOD   "**Spirit of God**" is another name for the **Holy Spirit**. The Spirit of God lives in people who believe in Jesus.

1 Corinthians 3:16

SPIRITUAL GIFTS   God gave each of us **spiritual gifts**. He gave us **special talents and skills** we can use to help others.

1 Corinthians 12:4–6

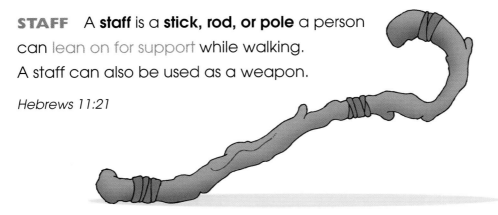

STAFF   A **staff** is a **stick, rod, or pole** a person can lean on for support while walking. A staff can also be used as a weapon.

Hebrews 11:21

Statute – Steward

STATUTE   A **statute** is a **rule, law, or decree** written down by a king.

1 Samuel 30:25

See also: Decree

STEADFAST   Joshua is **steadfast**. Joshua is strong and brave. He **will not change the things he believes**.

1 Corinthians 15:58

STEPHEN   **Stephen** was a good man—full of faith, God's grace, the Holy Spirit, and power.

He helped the disciples **spread the good news all over the world**. The religious leaders stoned Stephen because he loved God and spoke His word.

Acts 6:1–7, 7:54–60

STEWARD   Joseph had a **steward**. Joseph had a **servant who took care of his belongings**—his home, money, land, and animals.

Genesis 43:19

A B C D E F G H I J K L M N O P Q R **S** T U V W X Y Z

STILL, SMALL VOICE   God spoke to Elijah in a **still, small voice**. He spoke with **a gentle whisper**.

God did not shout or sound like an earthquake, a mighty wind, or a raging fire.

Elijah had to be quiet on the inside if he wanted to hear God's voice.

1 Kings 19:9–18

STONING   **Stoning** was a way of punishing people in Bible times. **Rocks were thrown at a person** until he died.

Numbers 15:35

STOREHOUSE   A **storehouse** is a **building used to store things**.

Joseph opened his storehouses and sold grain to the Egyptians.

Genesis 41:56

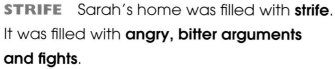

Strife – Sulfur

STRIFE   Sarah's home was filled with **strife**. It was filled with **angry, bitter arguments and fights**.

Proverbs 20:3, 30:33

STUMBLING BLOCK   Sarah's bad temper is a **stumbling block** to her friendship with Ann. It is **something that gets in the way**. Sarah's temper makes it hard for Ann to want to be her friend.

Romans 14:13

SUCCOTH   **Succoth** was the **name of two cities in the Bible**. Jacob lived in one. Moses and the Israelites camped in another on their way to the Promised Land.

Genesis 33:17; Exodus 12:37

SULFUR   **Sulfur** is a **bright yellow material**, like a stone or a crystal, that is easily set on fire. In Bible times, sulfur was known as brimstone.

Luke 17:29

See also: Fire and Brimstone

SWADDLING CLOTHES   Mary wrapped her baby in **swaddling clothes**.

She wrapped her baby in long **strips of soft cloth** to keep him quiet and still.

Luke 2:12

SWINE   **Swine** is another name for **pigs**.

Matthew 7:6

SYNAGOGUE   A **synagogue** is a **place where Jewish people meet to worship God** and learn from His Word. Jesus taught in a synagogue.

Matthew 9:35

TABERNACLE
The Children of Israel worshipped in the **Tabernacle**. The Tabernacle was like a **large tent surrounded by a fence**. The Tabernacle and everything in it could be moved from place to place.

Exodus 26–27

The Tabernacle ▶

TABITHA
Tabitha was **a disciple**. She always did good and helped the poor. One day she became sick and died. But Peter prayed and God raised her from the dead!

Acts 9:36–43

TABLET
A **tablet** is a special **surface to write on**. God gave Moses the Ten Commandments on two stone tablets.

Exodus 31:18

Tt

TALENT   A **talent** is an amount of **money measured by its weight**.

Exodus 37:24; Matthew 25:15

TARES   While the farmer slept, an enemy came and planted **tares** among his wheat. An enemy came and planted **weeds** in the farmer's field.

Matthew 13:24–30

TARSHISH   Jonah got on a boat bound for **Tarshish**. He was trying to run away from God.

God had told Jonah to go east across the desert to the city of Nineveh.

But Jonah got on a boat going west to a **port city** hundreds of miles the other way!

Jonah 1:1–3

That Way
Tarshish

Tarsus – Teacher

TARSUS   **Tarsus** was the **home of the apostle Paul.**
Tarsus is a town near the Mediterranean Sea.
Today, Tarsus is in the country of Turkey.

Acts 21:39

TAX GATHERER   A **tax gatherer** was
a **man who collected taxes** from the people.

He took people's money and
gave it to the government.

Luke 7:34, 9:2

TEACHER   Jesus is our **teacher**. Jesus is the
person who shows us and tells us how
to be the people God wants us to be.

Mark 10:17

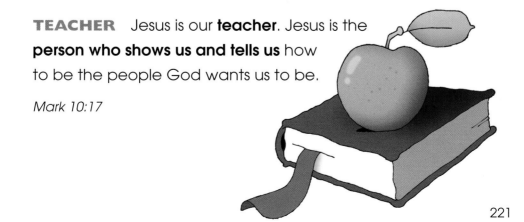

TEACHERS OF THE LAW   The **teachers of the law** taught God's children to obey the Law of Moses. But they were **proud teachers with hard hearts**. The chief priests and the teachers of the law wanted to kill Jesus.

Mark 11:18; 1 Timothy 1:7

TEMPLE   The **temple** was the **Jewish people's church in Jerusalem**.

King Solomon built the first temple with lots of gold inside. Two other temples were built later, in the same place.

The people of Israel came to Jerusalem to worship God at the temple.

1 Kings 6:1–38

TEMPTATION   **Temptation** is the **desire to do something foolish, wrong, or unwise**. It is wanting to do that wrong thing very, very much.

Matthew 6:13

Tt

TEN COMMANDMENTS   These are God's **Ten Commandments**. These are His **rules to all people** at all times:

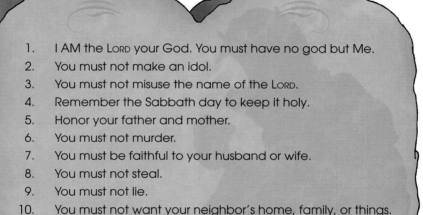

1. I AM the LORD your God. You must have no god but Me.
2. You must not make an idol.
3. You must not misuse the name of the LORD.
4. Remember the Sabbath day to keep it holy.
5. Honor your father and mother.
6. You must not murder.
7. You must be faithful to your husband or wife.
8. You must not steal.
9. You must not lie.
10. You must not want your neighbor's home, family, or things.

Exodus 20:1–17

TENT   The children of Israel lived in **tents**. They lived in **shelters made of cloth or animal skins** held up by ropes and poles. Tents can be moved from place to place.

Numbers 1:52

TENT OF MEETING   "**Tent of meeting**" is another name for the **Tabernacle**. Moses and the people of Israel worshiped God at the tent of meeting.

Exodus 40:2

A B C D E F G H I J K L M N O P Q R S **T** U V W X Y Z

Tt

TEREBINTH   Abram pitched his tents near the **terebinth** trees of Mamre.

He set up his tents near **tall, strong trees** in Mamre near the city of Hebron.

Genesis 13:18

TESTAMENT   A **testament** is an agreement between God and His children. Like a covenant, it is a **promise that can never be broken**.

Matthew 26:28; Hebrews 9:15

See also: Covenant, New Testament, Old Testament

TESTIFY   I will **testify** about my love for Jesus. I will **tell people** about God's love and the good things he has done!

John 1:34

Thicket – Thirty Pieces of Silver

THICKET   A **thicket** is a place of **tangled trees or bushes**. Abraham found a ram stuck in a thicket.

Genesis 22:13

THIEF ON THE CROSS   Jesus was crucified between two thieves. One thief mocked and insulted Him. The other **thief on the cross** knew he had done wrong and asked to be forgiven. Jesus told that thief, "Today you **will be with Me in paradise**."

Luke 23:39–43

THIRTY PIECES OF SILVER   Judas Iscariot was paid **thirty pieces of silver** to betray Jesus. He betrayed Jesus for thirty **small, silver coins**.

Matthew 26:14–15

See also: Betray

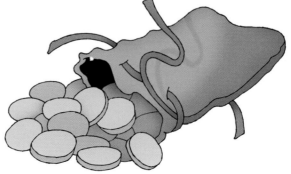

225

THOMAS   Thomas was **one of Jesus' disciples**.

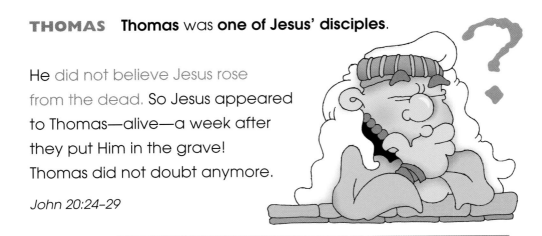

He did not believe Jesus rose from the dead. So Jesus appeared to Thomas—alive—a week after they put Him in the grave! Thomas did not doubt anymore.

John 20:24-29

THORN IN THE FLESH   A **thorn in the flesh** is a **kind of problem people face**. The apostle Paul had a thorn in the flesh. He said the problem kept him humble.

2 Corinthians 12:7

THRESHING   The farmer was **threshing** his grain.

The farmer was **beating his grain** to separate the seeds from the husks and straw.

Leviticus 26:5

See also: Winnowing

THRESHING FLOOR   A **threshing floor** is the **hard, flat surface where a farmer threshes his grain**.

Ruth met Boaz on the threshing floor.

Ruth 3:3

THRONE   The king sat upon his **throne**.

He sat on a **beautiful chair** at the top of a **small set of steps**. Like a crown or a scepter, the throne shows people the power of the king.

Revelation 7:10

TIMOTHY   **Timothy** was a **friend of the apostle Paul**. Timothy was a pastor and missionary. Paul wrote two letters to Timothy, which became books of the Bible.

1 Timothy 1:1–2

227

Tt

TITHE   David put his **tithe** in the offering basket at church. David gave **some of the money he made** back to God. David was thankful for God's blessings, and God rewarded him for it.

Malachi 3:10

THIS IS A TEST

"Bring your whole tithe into the storehouse so there will be food in my house. Test me and see!" says the Lᴏʀᴅ Almighty. "I will throw open the floodgates of heaven and pour out so much blessing you won't have room to take it all in."

Malachi 3:10

TOMB   Lazarus stood up and walked out of his **tomb**. Lazarus walked out of his **grave**. Jesus raised him from the dead!

John 11:38

TONGUES   The apostles spoke in **tongues**. God made it possible for the apostles to speak in **languages they did not know**.

Acts 2:4

TONGUES OF FIRE When God sent the **Holy Spirit** to Jesus' followers, He looked like **tongues of fire** dancing above their heads. Those little flames showed the people that the Holy Spirit had arrived. Then Jesus' followers started speaking in other languages!

Acts 2:1–4

TOWER OF BABEL The people of Babylon tried to build the **tower of Babel**. They tried to build a tall **building that reached all the way to heaven**.

The people of Babylon did not love or worship the one true God. So God mixed up their speech. He made them talk in different languages. They could not finish the tower of Babel.

Genesis 11:1–9

TRADITIONS The Pharisees set aside God's commands and followed their own **traditions**.

The Pharisees ignored God's Word and did **things their people had done for a long time**. Nobody knows, cares, or can remember why.

Mark 7:8

Tt

TREASURE IN HEAVEN   Jesus said, "Do not store up treasure here on earth. Store up **treasure in heaven**." Jesus said **a heart filled with God's goodness and love** is worth far more than any amount of money. It cannot be lost. And nothing can ever take it away.

Matthew 6:19–20

TREE OF LIFE   The **tree of life** was a special **tree in the Garden of Eden**. Eating fruit from the tree of life would make you live forever! At the end of time, God will have another tree of life in His new Jerusalem.

Genesis 2:9; Revelation 22:1–2

TREE OF THE KNOWLEDGE OF GOOD AND EVIL

God put two **special trees in the middle of the Garden of Eden**. One was the tree of life. The other was the **tree of the knowledge of good and evil.**

God told Adam and Eve not to eat from the tree of the knowledge of good and evil. He said, "If you eat from this tree, you will surely die."

Genesis 2:17

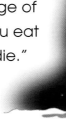

230

TRIBULATION   **Tribulation** is a time of, or something that causes, **great trouble and suffering**.

Revelation 7:14

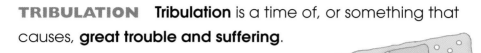

TRINITY   The **Trinity** is another name for the **One True God who is alive in three persons**. The three parts of the Trinity are God the Father, Jesus His Son, and the Holy Spirit.

Deuteronomy 6:4; 1 Corinthians 6:11, 8:6; Hebrews 1:8

TRIUMPHAL ENTRY   **Jesus rode a donkey into Jerusalem.** That special ride was called the **triumphal entry.** People cheered for Jesus and spread palm branches along the road as he came into the city.

Matthew 21:1-11

231

TRUST   **Trust** is the **confident belief**
that someone can and will do what they say.

John 14:1

TRUTH   Here is the **truth**.
Here is **the way things really are**.
God's word is the truth.

John 14:6, 16:13, 17:17

TUNIC   Titus wore a **tunic** to the temple.
Titus wore a **loose fitting garment**, with a wide
neck, that came down to his knees.

Matthew 5:40

Turban – Twelve Spies

TURBAN   A **turban** is like a **hat**. It is is made by winding a long cloth around a person's head.

Israel's high priest wore a turban.

Exodus 28:4

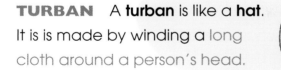

TWELVE DISCIPLES   The **twelve disciples** were the **men Jesus chose to follow Him**. Peter, Andrew, James, John, Philip, Bartholomew, Thomas, Matthew, James the son of Alphaeus, Judas the son of James, Simon the Zealot, and Judas Iscariot helped spread the good news about Jesus all over the world.

Luke 6:13–16

TWELVE SPIES   Moses sent **Twelve Spies** to see if God's children could take the Promised Land. Moses sent **twelve men who sneaked through the land.**

Ten spies were too afraid to try. The land was filled with giants! But Joshua and Caleb were not afraid. They said, "We can surely do it!"

Numbers 13–14; Joshua 14:6–12

233

Tt

Twelve Tribes – Two-Edged Sword

TWELVE TRIBES OF ISRAEL   The **twelve tribes of Israel** are **the families of Jacob's twelve sons**: Asher, Benjamin, Dan, Gad, Issachar, Joseph, Judah, Levi, Naphtali, Reuben, Simeon, and Zebulun.

Genesis 49:1–28

TWO-EDGED SWORD   **God's Word** is a **two-edged sword**. God says His Word can cut through people's thoughts and desires.

Hebrews 4:12

Uu

Unclean – Uz

UNCLEAN   God told the Israelites that some foods were **unclean**. He said eating them **went against God's commands**. Eating snakes and lizards was unclean. Eating chicken, fish, and sheep was clean.

Leviticus 11:46–47

UNLEAVENED BREAD   **Unleavened bread** is bread made without leaven. It is **bread made without yeast** so it will not rise up into a loaf. The Israelites ate unleavened bread.

Exodus 12:20

UPPER ROOM   Jesus and his disciples ate the Last Supper in the **upper room**. They celebrated the Passover in a **large guest room on the second floor** of a house in the city of Jerusalem.

Mark 14:15

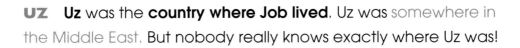

UZ   **Uz** was the **country where Job lived**. Uz was somewhere in the Middle East. But nobody really knows exactly where Uz was!

Job 1:1

V

VALLEY OF DRY BONES   Ezekiel saw the **Valley of Dry Bones**. Ezekiel saw **a vision of God's people**. Their hope had dried up.

They were sad and afraid. But God told Ezekiel He would put His Spirit in them. They would live again!

Ezekiel 37:1–14

VANITY   **Vanity**. Vanity. All is vanity! What's the use? Why should I care? It's all a **hopeless, empty, waste of time**.

Ecclesiastes 1:2

VASHTI, QUEEN   **Vashti** was the **queen of Persia**. She was the wife of King Xerxes.

Xerxes told Vashti to put on her crown and show everyone her beauty. But she disobeyed the king! So Xerxes became angry and **made Esther queen instead**.

Esther 1:12

VEIL   A **veil** is a **covering**.

Sometimes, a woman wears a veil over her face. There was also a veil in God's temple. It covered the holy of holies. When Jesus died, this heavy curtain tore from top to bottom. Through Jesus, anyone could come into God's holy place!

Matthew 27:51

VINE AND THE BRANCHES   The **vine and the branches** are **Jesus and His followers**. Jesus said, "I am the vine and you are the branches."

John 15:1–8

VINEDRESSER   A **vinedresser** is a farmer who **takes care of grape vines** in a vineyard. He looks after them day and night to make sure they grow big and strong.

John 15:1

VINEYARD   A **vineyard** is a **farm that grows grapes**.

Grapes grow on grape vines.

Genesis 9:20; Matthew 20:4

VIPER   A **viper** is a poisonous **snake**.
Once, a viper bit the apostle Paul.
But God kept the poison from hurting him!

Acts 28:3–6

VISION   God gave Daniel a **vision**.

Daniel saw **pictures in his mind** that had a message for God's people. Some visions show something that is yet to come.

Daniel 2:19

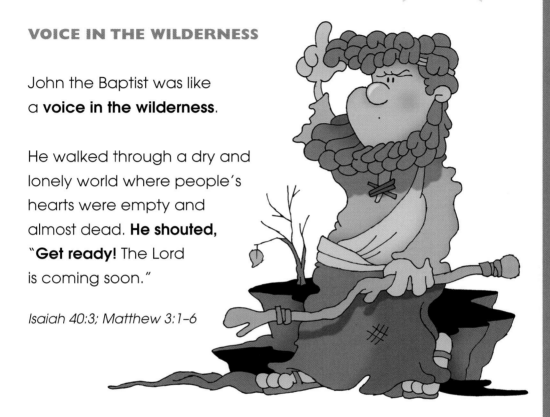

VOICE IN THE WILDERNESS

John the Baptist was like a **voice in the wilderness**.

He walked through a dry and lonely world where people's hearts were empty and almost dead. **He shouted, "Get ready! The Lord is coming soon."**

Isaiah 40:3; Matthew 3:1–6

VOID   The earth was formless and **void**. It was **completely empty**. It had nothing in it or on it at all.

Genesis 1:2

VOW   A **vow** is a **promise to God**. The Bible says if you make a vow, you need to keep it!

Ecclesiastes 5:4

A B C D E F G H I J K L M N O P Q R S T U V W X Y Z

W

WAGES **Wages** are the **payment** a person gets for the things he does.

Proverbs 10:16; Romans 6:23

WALKING ON THE WATER When the disciples saw Jesus **walking on the water**, they were afraid. But Jesus said, "Fear not!" He walked across the lake and got into the boat.

How did he do it? It was **a miracle**!

God is more powerful than any storm.
No wind is too strong. No wave is too high.
Jesus can help you wherever you are.
All you have to do is call out His name.

Matthew 14:22–33; John 6:19

See also: Miracle

WANDER Fuzzy little sheep love to **wander** off. They love to **walk slowly from here to there**, twisting and turning, drifting along wherever their little legs happen to take them.

Matthew 18:12

Watchman – Wedding Banquet

WATCHMAN   A **watchman** is a person who **guards a house or city**.

God said that His prophets were like watchmen for the whole country of Israel.

Ezekiel 3:17

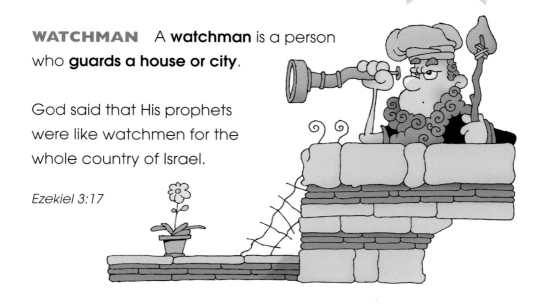

WAY, THE   Jesus said, "I am **the way**, the truth, and the life." He said, "I am the **one and only road that leads to heaven**."

John 14:6

WEDDING BANQUET   William went to a **wedding banquet**. He went to a **large meal** to celebrate a marriage.

Matthew 22:2–14; Luke 14:7–11

WELL Isaac's servants dug a **well**.

They dug a **deep hole** to try to find water.

Genesis 26:32

WHALE A **whale** is a **large sea creature**. God made whales on the fifth day of creation. Jonah was swallowed by a whale when he tried to run away from God.

Matthew 12:40

WHEAT Pete loves to eat **wheat**. He loves to eat the **grain** we use to make bread, cereal, pasta, and flour.

Exodus 29:2

242

Whirlwind – Widow

WHIRLWIND A **whirlwind** is a long, swirling finger of air, like a **tornado**. A whirlwind twists and spins around wrecking everything in its path.

Hosea 8:7

WICKED Wilma is **wicked**. She loves to think, say, and do **awful, terrible, evil** things that break God's heart.

Genesis 13:13

WIDOW A **widow** is a **woman whose husband has died**.

God told His people to take care of widows.

Deuteronomy 14:29

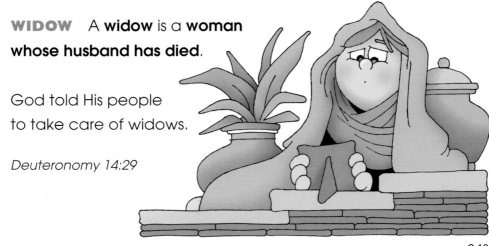

243

WIDOW'S MITE   A **mite** is a **small coin**, like a penny, that is worth almost nothing. A poor widow put two small mites in the offering. She gave everything she had.

Mark 12:41–44

The widow's two small mites ➤

WINE   **Wine** is a **drink** made from the juice of grapes. Jesus turned water into wine.

John 2:1–11

WINEPRESS   A **winepress** is a large **container used to press grapes** to make wine.

To make wine, the winepress was filled with grapes. Then someone would get inside and step on the grapes with their bare feet to squeeze out the juice.

Matthew 21:33

Wineskin – Wisdom

WINESKIN   Wallace poured wine into a **wineskin**. He poured wine into an **animal-skin bottle**.

Matthew 9:17

WINNOWING   Boaz was **winnowing** barley on the threshing floor.

He was **separating grain from the straw** by tossing it into the air with a rake.

Ruth 3:2

WISDOM   **Wisdom** is two important things: **knowing what God says and choosing to do it**.

Psalm 90:12

Ww

WISE MEN   **Wise men** followed the star and brought gifts to baby Jesus. **Godly men from the east** came and gave Jesus gold, frankincense, and myrrh. The wise men are also known as magi.

Matthew 2:1–12

WITNESS   A **witness** is someone who **tells what he or she knows**. Witnesses tell what they have seen or heard. Jesus wants His followers to be witnesses about Him. He wants Christians to tell others about what He's done.

Acts 1:8

WOE   Wilbur's heart was filled with **woe**.

Wilbur has **many terrible troubles**. He is sad, upset, and worried sick.

Proverbs 23:29

WOMAN AT THE WELL   Jesus gave the **woman at the well** a drink of living water. **She had an empty heart** that Jesus filled with words of life.

John 4:4–42

WORD OF GOD   **The Bible** is the **Word of God**. It is the living, breathing, light and life of Jesus Christ. Every word it says is true!

Revelation 19:13

IN THE BEGINNING!

In the beginning was the Word, And the Word was with God, and the Word was God. He was with God in the beginning. Through him all things were made; without him nothing was made that has been made. In him was life, and that life was the light of men.

John 1:1–4

WORKS   **Works** are the **things you do**. God wants His children to do good works. He wants His children to love others, share, and help each other.

Ephesians 2:10

Ww

WORSHIP   Willie loves to **worship** God.

He loves to **say I love you to God**.
He loves to thank God for all the
wonderful things He has done.

Psalm 99:9

WRATH   A gentle answer turns away
wrath. Kind words put out the fire of
a heart that burns with **anger**.

Proverbs 15:1

WRITING ON THE WALL   Belshazzar was the king of Babylon.

Like his father Nebuchadnezzar, Belshazzar was a very naughty
king. He saw the **writing on the wall**. He saw **God's hand write
four mysterious words** on the wall of his palace.

Belshazzar could not read the words. His magicians could
not read them either. But Daniel knew what they meant.
"Your days are numbered. Your kingdom has come to an
end!" he read. Belshazzar was killed that very night, and
Darius became the new king!

Daniel 5:1–31

Xerxes

XERXES

Xerxes was a **king in the land of Persia**.
He was the ruler of the land of Persia.

King Xerxes had a helper named Haman. Haman was a very bad man. He wanted the king to kill all the Jewish people.

But Queen Esther convinced Xerxes that it was wrong to kill God's chosen people.

So the king did not kill God's chosen people. He killed Haman instead.

Esther 1–10

See also: Chosen People, Esther, Haman, Mordecai, Vashti, Queen

Yy

YAHWEH **Yahweh** is a Hebrew **name for God**. It is a name for God in the language of the Jewish people. In English Bibles, Yahweh is printed as LORD or Jehovah.

Isaiah 12:2

YESHUA **Yeshua** is the Hebrew **name for Jesus**. It is Jesus' name in the language of the Jewish people. Yeshua means "salvation."

Matthew 1:21

YOKE A **yoke** is a **collar that holds two animals together**.

Matthew 11:29–30

See also: Ox

An ox yoke ➤

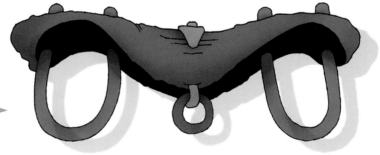

YOKEFELLOW Epaphroditus was Paul's **yokefellow**. He was Paul's **very close friend**.

Philippians 2:25, 4:2–3

Zacchaeus – Zacharias

ZACCHAEUS **Zacchaeus** was a **tax collector** in the city of Jericho. He was a tiny, little man who took people's money and gave it to the government.

One day a crowd gathered to hear Jesus speak. Zacchaeus climbed a tree so he could see. Jesus saw Zacchaeus in the tree. He asked to visit his home later that day. Zacchaeus was a selfish, greedy man. But when he met Jesus, he was converted. Jesus changed his heart.

Luke 19:1–10

ZACHARIAS **Zacharias** was the **father of John the Baptist**. He was a priest in Jerusalem. He helped people worship God at the temple.

When an angel told Zacharias he would have a son, Zacharias did not believe. He could not speak until John was born!

Luke 1:5–25, 57–80

Zz

A B C D E F G H I J K L M N O P Q R S T U V W X Y Z

Zeal – Ziggurat

ZEAL King David said, "The **zeal** for your house consumes me!" He said, "**Love and passionate devotion** for God fills my heart and mind."

Psalm 69:9; John 2:16–17; Romans 12:11

ZEBEDEE, SONS OF **James and John** were the **sons of Zebedee**. They were disciples of Jesus.

Mark 1:19–20

ZIGGURAT The people of Babylon tried to build a **ziggurat**. They tried to build a tower, like a **pyramid with four sides and many steps**.

The tower of Babel was probably a ziggurat.

Genesis 11:3–4

See also: Babylon, Tower of Babel

252

Zion – Zither

ZION **Zion** is another name for the **city of Jerusalem**. It can also mean the whole land of Israel.

2 Samuel 5:7

ZIPPORAH **Zipporah** was **Moses' wife**. She was married to Moses.

Zipporah and Moses had two sons, Gershom and Eliezer.

Exodus 18:1–5

See also: Moses

ZITHER Shadrach, Meshach, and Abednego heard the sound of a **zither**.

They heard a **stringed instrument** like a harp plucked with fingers or a pick.

Daniel 3:1–15

Zz

ZOPHAR **Zophar** was one of **Job's friends**. He tried to comfort Job and make him feel better.

Zophar told Job the terrible things that happened to him were God's punishment for all his sins. But Zophar's words were not God's words. So the things he said only made Job feel worse!

Job 2:11

ZOPHAR'S WORDS

Eliphaz, Bildad, and Zophar were Job's friends. They wanted to help. But the things they said didn't help Job at all. Why not?

Job's friends cared about him very much. They were smart. The things they said made perfect sense—but their words were not God's words. And God's words are the only words that can help anyone with anything!

Do you know someone who needs a helping hand today? Love them no matter what they say or do. Try your best to be a friend. Speak God's words with kindness and love. Jesus can change the hardest of hearts. He will make everything new.

If anyone is in Christ, he is a new creation; old things have passed away; behold, all things have become new.

2 Corinthians 5:17 NKJV

Map of the Holy Land

Philippi •

Tyre •

Capernaum •   • Sea of Galilee

Mount Carmel ▲   Cana •

Nazareth •

Cesarea •

Jordan River •

Samaria •

Bethel •

Emmaus •   • Jericho

Jerusalem •   ▲ Mount of Olives

▲ Mount Moriah

▲ Mount Nebo

Bethlehem •

Dead Sea •

Canaan

Moab

Israel

Egypt

Edom

Midian

Once upon a time, Phil A. Smouse wanted to be a scientist.

But scientists don't get wonderful letters and pictures from friends like you. So Phil decided to draw and color instead! He and his wife live in southwestern Pennsylvania. They have two children they love with all their heart.

Phil loves to tell kids like you all about Jesus. He would love to hear from you today! So get out your markers and crayons, and send a letter or a picture to:

Phil A. Smouse
Barbour Publishing, Inc.
1810 Barbour Drive
Uhrichsville, OH 44683

Or visit his website at www.philsmouse.com
and send him an e-mail at phil@philsmouse.com.